Giuseppe Zanini

The book of
HOW

DEAN

Contributors:
Andrea Bonanni   Pinuccia Bracco
Glauco Pretto

Text adapted by
Christine Casley

This edition first published in 1986 by
Deans an imprint of
The Hamlyn Publishing Group Limited
Bridge House, 69 London Road, Twickenham,
Middlesex TW1 3SB
London · New York · Sydney · Toronto

Text copyright © Arnoldo Mondadori Editore, Milano, 1973, 1986
This edition text copyright
© The Hamlyn Publishing Group Limited
1974, 1986
Illustrations copyright © The Hamlyn Publishing Group Limited
1974, 1986

ISBN 0 603 00469 5

Printed in Czechoslovakia
52112

INTRODUCTION

This book is a collection of brief but comprehensive outlines on a broad range of subjects that a child might study at school. These subjects, however, have been presented in a different manner with the emphasis on the unusual.

In an attempt to cover all fields of human knowledge, the problem has been which subjects to choose and which to omit so as to produce a book that would be comprehensive and yet not too daunting to the young reader. It was decided, therefore, not to adopt any fixed system but to present the material as a miscellany of curious or strange facts that would capture the child's attention, persuade him to read on and, in this way, broaden his horizons. The decision was based on the conviction that any knowledge acquired spontaneously and willingly becomes the most lasting.

The only connecting thread throughout this book, therefore, is the child's curiosity. The subject matter has been treated as simply as possible. The sole aim of the book is to give broad and basic answers without going into too many complex and technical details that might bore the child. It is hoped that the child will become more interested in the various subjects so that he will then study them individually in greater detail by himself.

CONTENTS

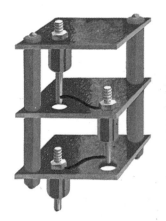

THE HOW OF PLANTS

Dionaea muscipula

Pinguicola

Nephentes alba marginata

Sarracenia

Byblis gigantea

How Linnaeus classified plants

As botanists gradually came to know more and more new plants after each great voyage of discovery, the need grew for a system in which all these plants could be put neatly into various groups. When we think of how many plants there are and how different they are from one another, we can see just how difficult it must have been to devise a way of classifying them.

The first scientist to carry out this great task was Carolus Linnaeus (1707–78), a Swedish naturalist. Linnaeus grouped plants according to their flowers and the number and type of stamens and pistils on these flowers.

Today, Linnaeus's classification has been replaced by newer and more accurate systems, but the achievement of Linnaeus remains great because he gave each plant two Latin names, The first name indicated the genus, or family, of the plant, and the second name gave the species, or particular member, of the family.

Linnaeus's system of naming plants is still used throughout the world today and at the major international botany congresses that are held every four years.

How the *Drosera* catches insects

Droseros is the Greek word for 'dewy' and the first thing that one notices about the *Drosera*, or sundew plant, is the sticky stem covered in soft, downy hair and scattered with glistening little bubbles that look like dewdrops. When insects see these 'dewdrops' they land on the plant for a drink. As soon as they touch the stem, the insects become stuck and the plant's downy hair curls round them like tentacles. The *Drosera* produces a liquid which breaks down the captured insects into food which the plant then absorbs.

The *Drosera* is, therefore, a carnivorous plant. It grows wild in damp places in Europe and North America and is about 20 centimetres high. One variety which occurs in Australia and South Africa reaches a height of one metre.

How the bladderwort catches its victims

Early in the summer pretty little bunches of golden-yellow flowers about a centimetre across appear floating on the water of ponds and ditches. This is the bladderwort, or *Utricularia*, a plant that keeps most of its body under water and looks very innocent. However underneath its leaves the *Utricularia* has lots of little bladders which turn into deadly traps should any unwary insect go too near them.

These bladders have a small opening surrounded by short hairs. When an insect explores the opening the plant swallows the insect and closes the opening with a special little lid. The plant then digests the captured animal through millions of microscopic tubes in its tissue.

This plant grows all over the world, on land as well as on the water, but the bulk of the species are found in tropical regions and only about four occur in Europe.

How pollen is made

All the higher forms of plant life reproduce themselves from seeds. These seeds are produced inside the flower of the plant after it has been fertilized. The stamens and the anthers are extremely important parts of the flower because they produce the pollen. Pollen is the very fine, yellow dust that comes away on the fingers whenever we touch the inside of a flower. These tiny yellow grains are one of the most precious substances in nature because they contain the secret of plant life.

It is pollen which fertilizes the ovary and sets off the process that finally produces the seeds. When pollen is examined under a microscope the minute specks of dust are enlarged and we can see the many different shapes of the individual grains which vary according to the plant of origin. Some pollen grains are oval, others are cylindrical and others are round. There are also pointed grains, some which are crescent-shaped and others with prickles on them.

The grains are smaller and flatter if the pollen comes from plants which are pollinated by the wind. This shape helps them to fly through the air. If the pollen is meant to be carried to other flowers by insects then the grains are larger and stickier.

How the *Nepenthe* of the tropical forests feeds itself

There are some seventy different varieties of *Nepenthe*, most of which grow in the tropical forests of Africa. These are rather strange plants which have clever traps

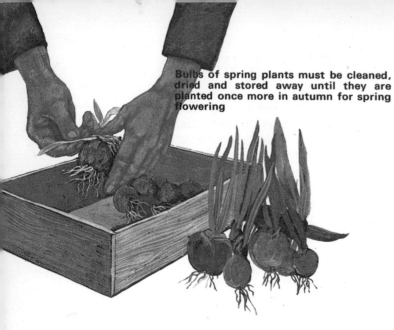

Bulbs of spring plants must be cleaned, dried and stored away until they are planted once more in autumn for spring flowering

How some plants can flower in the snow

One of the plants that flowers when the snow is still lying on the ground is the snowdrop.

The reason why this pretty little white flower can appear so early in the year, despite the cold weather, is the bulb from which it grows.

This bulb lies under the ground

to catch insects and other small creatures who are unwary enough to venture close to them.

The *Nepenthe* is a climbing plant which produces flowers in bunches. The plant's insect-traps are located at the tip of the leaves. These traps are an extension of the main vein of the leaf and look like stems with a small bladder on the end. This bladder is known as the ascidium and insects are attracted by its colour and its sugary contents. The insects go inside the ascidium but they cannot get out again because of hundreds of little stiff, downward-pointing hairs. Below these is a highly polished area, without hairs, which is like a greased slide. The more the insect struggles, the farther down it slips until it drowns in an evil-smelling liquid.

Galanthus nivelis or snowdrop

Winter aconite

Spring crocuses should be planted to produce patches of colour

and out of reach of the frost. It uses whatever warmth is left in the soil and when the air becomes warmer outside it sends out green leafy shoots.

The snowdrop is about 10 to 20 centimetres high. The petals that form the corolla have a small green spot at the end.

Snowdrops are common in meadows, along the banks of streams and in woods and forests.

How plants protect themselves from frost

Some plants are killed by the frost when winter arrives but the seeds they dropped on the ground in the autumn ensure that new plants grow to replace them in the spring.

Other plants spread out their leaves and flatten them against the ground in order to obtain whatever warmth is left in the soil. The violet is a plant that does this.

Myrtle and heather allow their upper plant to wither and die, but the lower part of the stem stays alive and produces buds when the growing season comes.

Many other plants escape from the cold weather by hiding under the soil. These plants are tubers, bulbs and roots which have stored up all the food they need. When the warm weather returns they are ready to push out green leaves and new buds.

Sometimes mechanical means are used to protect plants from frost. In regions where citrus fruits are grown oil heaters, called smudge pots, are placed in the groves and huge fans are also used to keep the air moving and prevent the cold air from settling on the fruit trees.

How conifers are protected from the frost

Not all trees shed their leaves in winter. Some have special defences which enable them to stand up to snow and ice. These trees are known as evergreens. One of the most common examples is the fir tree, better known as the Christmas tree.

Fir trees look extremely pretty when they are covered in snow, but the snow does not remain on them for long. The branches of the fir tree are made to bend under a weight and when the snow becomes too heavy the branch sags downwards and the snow slides off. This is how the fir tree protects itself against the weight of snow that falls in the mountains and which would otherwise crush the tree.

Conifers are so well protected from the rigours of winter that they can wear their beautiful green foliage when the weather is bitterly cold. The leaves of conifers are as thin as needles and covered in a special substance which protects them from the frost. This substance also prevents excessive evaporation of the moisture from the leaf which would cause the leaf to wither and drop off.

When the branch of a conifer is broken the wound is soon covered with a waterproof resin which heals the scar. This resin, which has an aromatic smell, is produced in large quantities by conifers.

Leaving aside food plants, conifers include some of our most useful plants. More than three-quarters of commercial timber is obtained from them and a large amount of coniferous wood is used as pulp in the manufacture of paper.

Gladiolus bulb

Iris root or rhizome

How plants catch diseases

Bacteria are tiny organisms that can be seen only through a microscope. They live alone as solitary individuals or in groups that are linked like chains. They vary in

Grapefruit canker caused by the bacterium *Phytomonas*

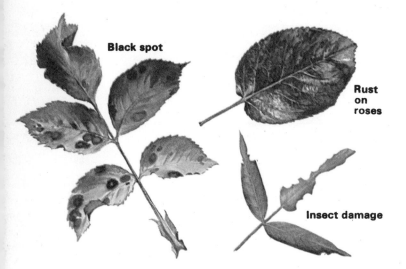

Black spot

Rust on roses

Insect damage

Rot on a carrot caused by the bacterium *Xanthomonas carotae*

shape according to their species.

Bacteria are responsible for many diseases in people, plants and animals. These diseases are infectious because they can be passed on whenever the bacteria move to a new place. In plants, over 150 different species of bacteria cause three main types of disease: vascular, parenchymatous and hyperplasic.

In vascular diseases the bacteria attack the vessels and main channels of a plant. This causes a blockage of vital food supplies and the plant dies.

In parenchymatous diseases, the bacteria attack the active tissues of the plant which then rots and dies.

In hyperplasia, the bacteria cause the cells of the plants to multiply wildly and produce swellings or tumours on the stem, the roots and sometimes even on the leaves.

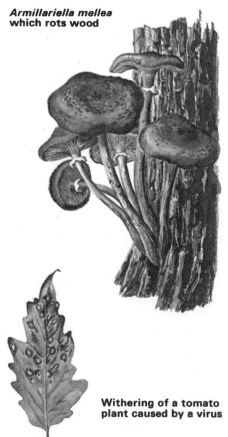

***Armillariella mellea* which rots wood**

Withering of a tomato plant caused by a virus

Plants can also catch serious diseases from viruses. There are many kinds of virus, each different from the other and each capable of causing several disorders. It has been found that viruses are carried from one plant to another by insects. These insects act as carriers by sucking the juices of a diseased plant and then injecting them into a healthy one.

A number of viruses are soil-borne and some of these are spread by eelworms that feed on plant roots.

Man, too, can spread viruses by handling diseased plants and then touching healthy ones.

One disorder caused by viruses is dwarfism when the plant is stunted. Other virus infections attack the leaves and make them dried and crumpled or cause blisters on the plant's tissues.

How plant diseases are fought

There are many diseases that can afflict plants. Some of these diseases produce symptoms that are clearly visible. Other diseases are more insidious and attack the plant from within. In this way they sap the strength of the plant and by the time the disease is discovered it is too late to save the plant.

These insidious diseases are the most difficult to study because it is practically impossible to see or know what is going on inside the plant. In some cases the disease is the result of different factors, each of which combines to cause several changes to take place.

In practice, some cures are more expensive than the plant itself and it is cheaper simply to let the plant die.

It is easier to tackle plant diseases when these have been caused by external factors. For example, there are many insects and other small creatures that bring about certain changes in plants. Once these changes are recognized, the disease can be treated by chemical and other means. Today helicopters and aeroplanes are used to spray insect-killing chemicals on crops which have been attacked by pests and parasites.

It is important to know the cause of the disease so that the cure can be found. Fortunately, modern botanists are helped by chemists using the most advanced forms of technology.

Probably the best control is provided by the use of disease-resistant plants and extensive efforts are being made to develop such varieties.

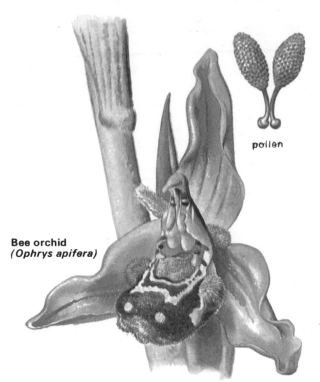

pollen

Bee orchid
(Ophrys apifera)

Sage
(Salvia
patens)

How a flower is made

A flower consists, first of all, of a pedicle, or stem, that joins it to the plant. The stem broadens out into a hollow cup known as the receptacle. This is surrounded by green sepals which form the calyx. The flower's petals grow from the calyx in all kinds of shapes and colours.

At the centre of the flower there is a part that resembles a long-necked bottle. This is the pistil. The top of the pistil is called the stigma, the neck is called the style and the bottom, which is wider than the rest, is the ovary. Inside the ovary lie several tiny grains called ovules. Each one of these grains will become a seed. The ovary around the seeds will grow larger and turn into a fruit. The pistil is surrounded by several thread-like filaments, the stamens. At the top of each stamen there is a bag-like structure called the anther which contains the pollen.

How cross-pollination of plants takes place

Everything inside a flower is arranged to make pollination possible. This operation involves the transfer of pollen from the anthers of the stamens to the pistil.

It is very rare, however, that the pollen produced by one flower is used to fertilize the pistil in the same flower. Instead, flowers are designed to obtain pollen from other plants and their flowers. This enables better seeds and fruits to be produced and is known as cross-pollination. Its usefulness was demonstrated by the great naturalist, Charles Darwin, in 1859.

Cross-pollinating flowers occasionally have their pollen waiting on the stamens before the pistil is ready to take it; or the pistil may be ready but the stamens have produced no pollen. Some plants produce flowers with stamens only (male flowers) while others produce flowers with only pistils (female flowers). These plants are pollinated with the help of the wind which blows the pollen grains through the air.

Such plants produce huge amounts of pollen because much of it is lost in the air and only a small quantity finally reaches its proper destination.

How plants attract insects for pollination

Some plants entrust their pollen to the winds. Others use water as a carrier and still others simply pollinate themselves. However in most cases the vital task of pollination is carried out by insects.

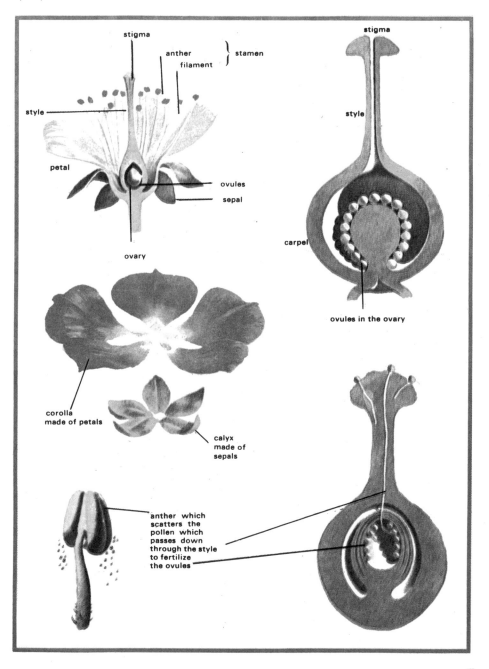

To attract insects plants produce flowers that have beautiful scents and colours. The shape of the flower's corolla, the part with the petals, is designed to let pollinating insects in but to keep out other unwelcome creatures.

Sometimes the pollinating mechanism inside a flower is amazingly complex. An example is the sage flower: when a bee is attracted by the scent or the nectar, it stands on the lowest petal to enter the flower. As it does so, the bee presses on a kind of lever which makes the flower's stamens come down and touch the hairy back of the bee, covering

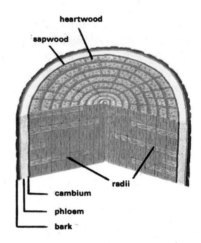

Diagram of a tree trunk showing the xylomatic, or woody, mass and the annual rings

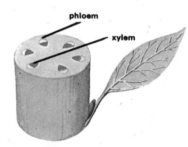

Cross-section of a stem showing the vessel structure at the rim

it with pollen. The bee then enters another flower and the whole operation is repeated.

The sage is one of those plants that lets its stamens ripen before its pistil. So when the bee lands on a flower where the stamens and the anthers have withered away, there is a pistil waiting to pick up the pollen from the bee's back to fertilize itself.

Cross-section of a root showing the central vascular tissue which supports the plant

How plants absorb water

Every plant has to feed itself in order to carry out its vital functions. Usually the raw materials are extracted from the surrounding soil through the roots. In this way the roots supply the leaves of the plant, which are really small chemistry laboratories, with water and the necessary minerals to produce organic substances.

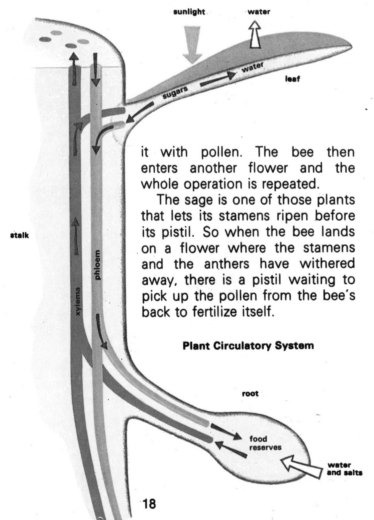

Plant Circulatory System

There are two basic types of roots: the taproot which consists of a single large axis from which fine hairs grow, such as the radish or the turnip, and the fasciculated root which is composed of several axes each of the same size, as in the dahlia.

In each type of root there is a root-cap at the end of each root. This cap protects the growing part of the root organism and helps it to dig into the soil. When viewed through a powerful magnifying glass these caps are seen to be covered in very fine hairs. It is through these hairs that the roots suck in water and certain mineral salts from the soil.

How the inside and outside of leaves are built

Leaves are usually made up of two parts. One of these parts is long and slender and called the stem or petiole. The stem joins the leaf to the main stalk of the plant. The other part of the leaf is flat and open and known as the blade or lamina. The blade is covered in veinings which represent the skeleton of the leaf. These veins link all the tiny 'laboratories' with other parts of the parent plant. If we hold a leaf up to the light we can see that underneath the main veining there is another denser and much smaller set of veining. These tiny veins contain the channels through which the water drawn in from the roots is distributed throughout the leaf.

The surface of the leaf is covered with many microscopic pores called stomata. The stomata absorb carbon dioxide from the air which is then used to build up carbohydrates, and allow water to evaporate.

How plants produce organic substances

By using water, air and some mineral substances obtained from the soil, plants produce sugar and starch which are the basis of all organic matter. This transformation is made possible by chlorophyll which takes the energy of

How plants feed

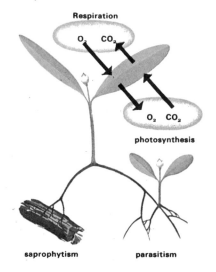

Respiration

O_2 CO_2

O_2 CO_2

photosynthesis

saprophytism   parasitism

Diagram showing the photosynthesis of chlorophyll

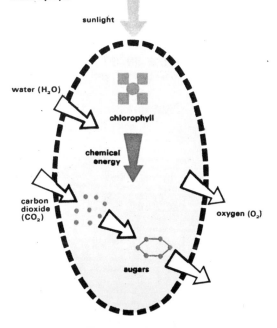

sunlight

water (H_2O)

chlorophyll

chemical energy

carbon dioxide (CO_2)

oxygen (O_2)

sugars

sunlight. Chlorophyll then uses this energy to separate the atoms of oxygen, hydrogen and carbon which make up air and water and rejoins them to produce organic matter and oxygen gas.

This process of photosynthesis is an extremely delicate and complicated operation. Scientists have succeeded in producing artificial photosynthesis.

How plants defend themselves from drought

Plants that grow in dry regions are known as xerophilous, a word which means they love dry places. The roots of these plants spread out horizontally close to the surface of the soil. In this way the roots can soak up whatever rain falls before the heat of the Sun evaporates all the moisture. Sometimes the roots of xerophilous plants go down deep into the soil to reach damper places or even a supply of water.

The stalks of xerophilous plants have no leaves and they are covered with a waxy material which prevents moisture from evaporating from the plant. These plants are also covered in sharp thorns or spines to stop animals from eating them.

In dry, desert areas these plants, and especially the cacti, are a precious source of water as well as food for living creatures. If they had no thorns to defend them they would all be eaten up by hungry and thirsty animals.

Many of these plants produce beautiful flowers and fruit after rain. The fruit can be eaten both by people and animals.

How the poison of stramonium acts

Stramonium, or the Jimson Weed is also known as 'the Devil's grass'. The plant got this name because its poison seems to drive the victim mad as if he were possessed by the devil.

The alkaloids in the plant can also cause serious distortion of the eyesight. In small doses, however, these poisons can be used to treat certain illnesses.

Stramonium found in certain drugs is extracted from the leaves

Philocactus

Lobivia

Neoporteria aspillaga

Opuntia microdasys

of this plant. It acts as a sedative and eases nerve and rheumatic pains. Stramonium leaves are also used to make special cigarettes for the treatment of asthma. The seeds of the plant provide an oil which is used in lotions to be rubbed on the body.

How the leaves of the prickly pear are made

The prickly pear grows wild in warm Mediterranean regions. It anchors itself to rocky, barren slopes and forms large areas of scrub that grow to about 3 metres high. On cultivated land the prickly pear is often cultivated as a hedge. It is enough to plant just one leaf for a whole bushy shrub to start growing.

'Leaf' is not really the correct word to describe the green, fleshy vegetation of this plant. The leaves are really parts of the plant's trunk which measure from 15 to 40 centimetres long and 15 centimetres wide.

The actual leaves of the prickly pear are very small and are shed almost as soon as they have appeared on the plant. They leave behind them thick tufts of thin needles. One of these needles grows outwards and becomes very sharp.

Since the prickly pear has no leaves the task of producing chlorophyll, without which no plant can live, is carried out by the trunk.

The prickly pear was introduced into Australia at the end of the eighteenth century as a food plant for cochineal insects. It spread and by 1870 had become a pest in Queensland and New South Wales. Its growth was controlled by the introduction of a little moth, the cactoblastis.

How truffles are found

The truffle is a strange fungus that grows from 5 to 10 centimetres below the ground. It can only be located by the peculiar smell it gives out and the best way to find it is to use a pig or a dog which has been trained in truffle hunting.

The dog or pig is taken to the place on a lead. As soon as it smells a truffle the animal is released and runs to the spot. The pig digs the truffle up with its nose; the dog uses its paws. The animals are rewarded with something to eat.

Some truffles are as big as a clenched fist but others are much smaller. There are two main types of truffle: the black and the white. The white truffle is much more sought after for its pungent and penetrating taste. It is a pale, dirty yellow in colour.

Astrophitum myriostigma

Trichocereus candicans

Mammillaria zeilmanniana

Hawarthia margarantifera

Cone of the *Picea abies*

Cone of the *Abies alba*

Picea abies

How to tell a silver fir from a red fir

The red fir or *Picea excelsa* is a native of northern Europe and also grows on the upper slopes of the Alps. The silver fir which has the botanical name *Abies alba*, grows on most mountain ranges of southern and central Europe at altitudes ranging from 800 to 1,500 metres.

The silver fir has a pale grey bark which is quite smooth when the tree is young, but it becomes roughened and darkened with age. The red fir has a rough, reddish-brown bark. The two trees have differently-formed cones: in the red fir they are pendulous and soft to the touch, but the silver fir's cones are hard and stick up vertically. Moreover, the needle-shaped leaves of the red fir grow in a spiral arrangement round the stem, whereas those of the silver fir are arranged in two files on the same level of the branch and the underparts are marked with two broad white lines. Many silver firs grow to more than 40 metres high.

How the rose of Jericho survives in the Sahara

The rose of Jericho, or resurrection plant, is a shrub consisting of several branches that lie on the ground to support the plant. These branches produce small leaves and flowers. When the burning desert Sun dries up all traces of moisture, the branches of the rose of Jericho roll up into a ball to protect the small fruit that contains the seeds.

When the rain returns the rose of Jericho unrolls its branches and scatters its seeds which are then ready to produce new plants.

How to tell the age of a tree

If we examine the trunk of a tree that has been chopped down, we will see first of all the outer ring of the bark which acts as a sort of waterproof coat for the tree. Inside the outer covering come a number of concentric rings.

Each one of these rings represents a year in the life of the tree. The space between the rings is the wood which the tree produced during one year.

By counting the number of rings we can tell when the tree was born. These rings also indicate the dry periods the tree lived through as well as wet periods. In dry times the rings are very thin. In heavy rainfall years the rings are thicker.

Slender cores of wood can be taken from a tree, from the bark to the centre of the trunk; these samples reveal the same information and are taken with a borer that does no significant damage to the tree.

How the pineapple grows

The pineapple plant produces large fruits and has a stalk that grows under the ground. This stalk pushes out a tuft of fleshy leaves which are up to a metre long and are prickly at the edges. From the centre of this crown of leaves there grows a stem which also has leaves growing on it. At the top of the stem there is a cluster-like flower of bluish blossoms.

When these flowers have bloomed the stem underneath them swells and produces the fruit which is sold fresh or in tins. Pineapple fruit can weigh up to 4 kilogrammes.

The top of the fruit has a tuft of leaves known as a crown. If the pineapple is placed in the ground in warm, moist conditions, this tuft of leaves will produce a new plant. This is one of the most common methods used to reproduce the fruit.

It was once fashionable to grow pineapples under glass in England, but this practice has now died out. Most pineapples are grown in Thailand. They are gathered unripe and allowed to ripen on the journey to their destination.

How to tell ebony from other woods

There are many trees that produce ebony. They belong to a family known as the Ebenaceae which grows in the tropical parts of Africa and Asia, especially India, Sri Lanka, and Malaysia. In Asia forests with trees of the Ebenaceae family are found up to altitudes of more than 1,500 metres.

The ebony tree has broad leaves and is very large. Its wood is exported throughout the world because of its many uses, but the tree also provides fruit which is quite pleasant and eaten locally.

The most commonly used ebony wood is black. It is also very hard and durable. But there are red and banded varieties of ebony, too. African ebony is brown with even black veining.

Ebony is used in making good-quality furniture, carvings and arts and crafts. These include black piano keys, walking sticks, golf club heads and knife handles. As ebony is a very hard and fine-grained wood it can be smoothed and polished to a high degree.

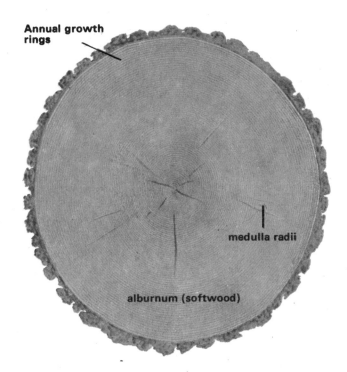

Annual growth rings

medulla radii

alburnum (softwood)

It is this polish that distinguishes ebony from such imitations as pear-wood that has been dyed black.

Timber prepared as props at a coal mine

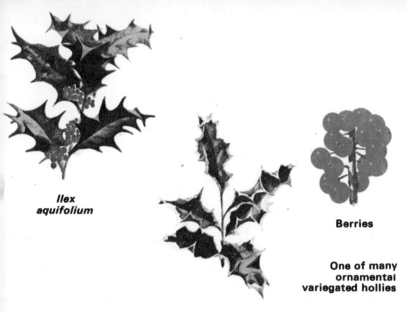

Ilex aquifolium

Berries

One of many ornamental variegated hollies

How cedar oil is made

Oil of cedar is a precious substance which the ancient peoples used to embalm dead bodies. It was also once used to coat books to preserve them from insects and damp. The oil is obtained by distilling it from the African cedar and is an 'essential' oil, that is one that gives a plant, flower or fruit its distinctive odour or flavour. These oils are used for the scenting or flavouring of numerous products, such as perfumes, cosmetics and soaps.

The African cedar grows in the north of that continent, especially on the Atlas Mountains. It is a very imposing conifer that bears many leaves and grows to a height of more than 40 metres. It closely resembles the more famous cedar of Lebanon which was also highly prized by the ancient peoples.

Cedarwood is soft and rich in resin. It can be worked easily and is used extensively in building and furniture-making.

How holly defends itself from animals

The holly bush can often look like a tree and grow to a height of more than 7 metres. Usually it is a shrub which in winter stands out in contrast with its glossy, green leaves against the dead, brown foliage all around it.

The leaves of holly are intended to keep animals away. The leaves on the lower branches of the plant are very prickly as this is the part most likely to be attacked by hungry animals. The leaves nearer the top of the plant are not so prickly because they are out of the reach of leaf-eating animals.

Holly usually grows in oak and chestnut woods. In winter the plant has bright red berries and is widely used in Christmas decorations.

How the *Arbutus* became the emblem of the Italian independence movement

The *Arbutus unedo*, or strawberry tree, became the emblem of the Carbonari, the band of patriots who fought for the independence of Italy during the 1800s. They chose this plant because it bore the colours of Italy: green leaves, white flowers and red berries.

The berries, which are pleasant to eat, ripen from September to December. The leaves of the *Arbutus* are usually dark-green but they turn a lighter shade in the autumn. The flowers appear after December.

Clover

Plantain

Common meadow plants

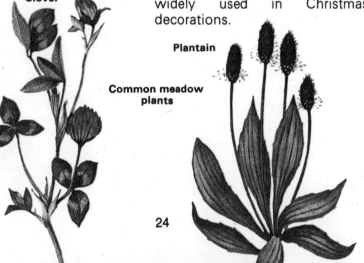

24

Leaves, flowers and fruit of the arbutus

How dates are used

Dates are used in many ways. Those with a soft, pulpy flesh provide a syrup known as date honey which can be made into a jam. Hard-fleshed dates can be preserved in sugar or made into flour. The juice of dates can be fermented and turned into an alcoholic drink called arrack. The leaves of the date palm can be used for making mats or cord. The seeds or stones of the dates can also be made into buttons.

How the cyclamen got its name

The plant known as the cyclamen got its name from the Greek word *cyclos* meaning 'circle'. This is a word that can be seen in 'bicycle' and 'tricycle' and it suits the cyclamen because, when the plant has finished flowering, the stalks tend to wind round in circles to resemble small springs, drawing the fruit down to the soil. They can be seen growing like this in woods and mountains of central Europe and the Mediterranean region.

The cyclamen belongs to the Primulaceae family and has about twenty species. Varieties include *Cyclamen neapolitanum* which has small pink flowers. Another variety the *Cyclamen persicum*, is a well-known florists' plant whose varieties have doubled, crested, shredded and greatly enlarged flowers of varying shades.

The cyclamen has broad, long-stalked leaves, usually heart- or kidney-shaped which in cultivated forms are often splashed or lined with white.

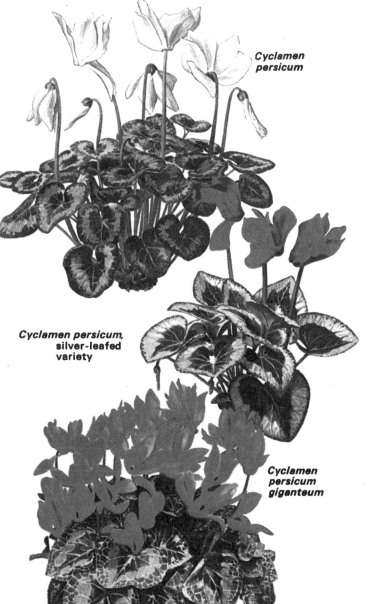

Cyclamen persicum

Cyclamen persicum, **silver-leafed variety**

Cyclamen persicum giganteum

THE HOW OF ANIMALS

How remoras can follow sharks

The remora, or shark-sucker, has always excited the wonder and curiosity of seafarers. This fish has a flat, oval disc on top of its head which it uses to fasten itself firmly to flat surfaces. This habit has earned the remora a certain reputation in legends.

In olden days sailors thought the remora had tremendous strength and could slow down and even stop a ship by fastening on to its keel. But these are only legends. The remora is about 40 centimetres long and could never stop any craft no matter how small.

Remoras merely use their suckers to be carried along by large fish. They usually choose sharks and stay attached to their underside during hunting expeditions. The remora then eats whatever is left over. Sometimes remoras swim along on their own power and hunt for food.

In some parts of the tropics fishermen have used remoras with a line attached to their tails to catch larger fish.

Remoras belong to the family Echeneidae. There are about seven species found in all tropical and temperate seas.

How animals are classified

In zoos the popular names of the animals on display are written on a label in front of their cages. The label also carries the animal's scientific name in Latin. For example, on a lion's cage, the Latin name is *Panthera leo*; on a tiger's cage the name is *Panthera tigris*; and on the cage of a leopard the name is *Panthera pardus*.

Latin is the language accepted by scientists and zoologists throughout the world to avoid confusion. The Latin name for any animal consists of two words because the scientific classification of animals still follows the basic principle laid down by the botanist Carolus Linnaeus. In the examples we have already quoted the first part of the names is the word *Panthera*: this refers to the genus of the animal. The second part of the name refers to the species. Members of an animal species that have many features in common come together in a genus. The *Panthera* genus, for example, includes the large cats which are unable to purr. Smaller cats, which can purr but do not roar, belong to the genus *Felis*. Both genera are in the family Felidae.

A number of genera form a family and several families form an order. The orders come together under classes and the classes fall into types. The total of all these forms the animal kingdom.

A remora attached to a shark

The ocean sunfish belongs to the family Molidae and can often be seen sunning itself or resting in the surface waters of temperate or tropical seas. Like the remora it belongs to the class of Teleostei.

Ocean sunfish

How the ocean sunfish is made

The ocean sunfish was known in ancient times but the first fishermen who caught these animals thought they were mutilated. This is because the sunfish has a very large head and appears to have no body.

On closer examination it can be seen that the sunfish does, in fact, have a body even though the tail has practically disappeared and the tail and anal fins have grown together into one unit.

The sunfish is a large animal and can measure more than 3 metres in length. It is flat and round in shape and can weigh as much as 2 tons.

Despite its large size it is not an animal of prey, feeding on small fishes and boneless creatures. It has a small mouth and does not swim very well, preferring to drift along in a current.

Classification of a dromedary

Kingdom	Animal
Phylum	Chordata
Class	Mammal
Order	Artiodactyla
Family	Camelidae
Genus	Camelus
Species	Dromedarius

How the condor became a symbol of freedom

There is an old tradition among the Indians of Lake Titicaca that dates back to the Spanish conquest of South America. It concerns the fight between a condor and a bull. The condor was the emblem of the Indians while the bull represented the Spanish conquerors. According to the story the condor was put into a sack with only its neck and head left free and the sack was then tied to the back of the bull. The condor began to peck savagely at the bull's head so that the bull lept about madly to get rid of its attacker.

The battle ended in victory for the condor to the applause of the Indians who saw in this duel a way of showing their dislike of their conquerors.

Condor of the Andes

How to tell seals from sea-lions

Many varieties of seals live beyond the Arctic Circle. All these animals have short necks and no external ears. It is this latter feature that distinguishes true seals from sea-lions which have prominent ears.

Seals range in size from the little fresh-water seal of Siberia, about one metre long, to the enormous sea elephant of the subantarctic regions, which can grow to 6 metres in length.

The most common type of seal, however, grows to a length of just over 2 metres. Its fur is brown or yellowish with dark patches. The seal's hind legs are part of its tail and cannot be used for walking. For this reason it moves by lunging its body along in a clumsy manner when on land.

On the ice the animal is not so awkward and it slides along for considerable distances. But the seal's true element is the sea for this animal is an extremely skilful swimmer and dives at the slightest sign of danger.

How turtles swim

It seems impossible that tortoises that move in such a slow, cumbersome manner should have relatives that swim fast through the ocean. Turtles, which very closely resemble tortoises, are sometimes as quick as fish in moving through the water, despite their heavy shell.

These turtles can weigh up to 250 kilogrammes but they have adapted wonderfully to aquatic life. Through living in the sea for millions of years, their bodies have become streamlined and their paws have turned into flippers.

**Sea turtle
(Chelonia mydas)**

It does this by leaping out of the water, bending itself almost double to do so. Many salmon die of sheer exhaustion while others are caught and devoured by such animals as bears.

When the fish has finally reached the fresh, clear waters of its destination, the female digs a pit in the stream gravel into which she lays her eggs. The male immediately fertilizes them and the female covers them with

Pacific salmon

Turtles come ashore only to lay their eggs. They drag themselves on to deserted beaches where they dig holes for their eggs.

Their home is the sea and that is where they find their food. Turtles eat meat or plants according to their species. The meat of the turtle itself is regarded as a delicacy, especially the green turtle of the Atlantic and Pacific Oceans.

The scientific name of turtles is Chelonia and they belong to the reptile class.

How the salmon passes waterfalls

The salmon lives near the coastline in the Atlantic and Pacific Oceans in the northern hemisphere. In the month of June it leaves the ocean and swims up the river to the place where it was born. The salmon looks for fresh water with plenty of oxygen in it. Nobody knows what makes the fish undergo such tremendous difficulties to complete its journey, but the salmon goes on and many of them die before their journey's end.

In its journey upstream the salmon has to get past waterfalls.

gravel. The Pacific salmon dies soon after spawning, but many Atlantic salmon return to the sea and may spawn again. Most spawning takes place in the late summer; the young are born about two or three months later and swim to the sea after about two years.

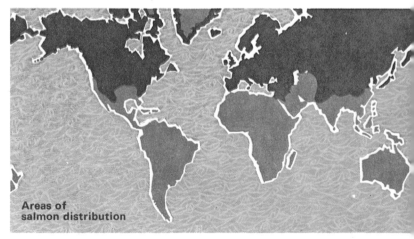

**Areas of
salmon distribution**

How the earthworm digs its tunnels

Earthworms cannot stand dry conditions in the soil: their bodies must always be in contact with damp earth and even a few minutes' exposure to the sunlight makes them dry up and die.

Earthworms spend most of their lives digging tunnels in the soil. It is quite surprising how they can burrow their way into even hard ground simply by using the strength of their muscles, for earthworms do not have any special physical equipment for digging.

They contract and expand in a rhythmic manner to force an aperture in the ground and then they push on with their head.

The earthworm swallows some of the soil he moves through. From it, the animal extracts food in the form of vegetable waste. The earthworm then expels the 'digested' soil and leaves it as a worm-cast. It has been estimated that the yearly deposition above ground of soil by earthworms is between 7 and 16 tons per acre in England.

Earthworms can grow up to 15 centimetres or more in length. In tropical countries some earthworms are as long as 2 metres.

How the buffalo defends itself from insect bites and stings

The buffalo likes to make its home in marshy places where it loves to roll in the mud and stay there for hours at a time. It does this for a very good reason: the mud dries into a hard crust all over the buffalo's skin and acts as a shield against the sting of insects and the burning rays of the Sun. This muddy protection allows the buffalo to live in the unhealthy atmosphere of marshes and swamps where no other type of cattle could survive.

The buffalo needs complete freedom. It could never work as a draft animal or live in a barn like domestic cattle.

Male and female
Banteng
(Bos banteng)

How beehives are organized

A large beehive can contain up to 80,000 bees but there is never any danger that such a vast number of insects will lead to confusion or chaos.

There is only one queen in a hive and her sole task is to keep on laying eggs. There are several hundred male bees, known as drones, who do no work except fertilize the eggs. But as soon as a new queen is born these drones are massacred by the worker bees who are all females, though incapable of laying eggs.

The worker bees form the overwhelming majority of the population of a beehive and collect all the nectar and pollen.

Bees suck the nectar from the flower through a special nose-tube and then carry it in a sack which contains up to 50 milligrams. The pollen is carried in two little baskets on the bee's hind legs. The worker bee delivers these ingredients and other worker bees in the hive mix them together into a sort of paste which is fed to the larvae so that they will develop into adult insects.

How the gardener-bird builds its nest

Little is known about the peculiar habits of the gardener-bird which has a marked liking for colourful objects and for what seems to be gardening. This bird lives in forest clearings in New Guinea. It builds an elaborate nest shaped like a little hut and surrounds it with a

Gaur *(Bos gauria)*

Water-buffalo *(Bubalus bubalis)*

Crestless gardener bird

sort of garden which it decorates with flowers, shells and various colourful objects. These objects are not just thrown together haphazardly: the gardener-bird very carefully arranges everything and tries it out in different patterns before deciding how the garden will look.

Related species of this bird can decorate the interior of their nests by painting them with colours which they make with their own saliva and various materials. Sometimes these birds even use 'brushes' made of small bunches of leaves.

How the ancestor of the horse developed

The illustrations on this page show the various stages in the evolution of the horse. The earliest ancestor of today's animal was *Eohippus* which lived about 50 million years ago. It stood only about 25 centimetres high and lived in the American prairies migrating from there to Asia and Europe where it bred rapidly. The *Orohippus* and *Mesohippus* appeared some 20 million years later and were bigger animals. But the first of these animals to look like today's horses was the *Parahippus*. The *Pliohippus*, which first appeared on Earth about 10 million years ago, bore an even closer resemblance to the horses of today.

How penguins hatch their eggs

During the mating season penguins gather together by the tens of thousands along the coasts of Antarctica. The female penguins lay one or two eggs which they place in a hollow in the ground. They take turns with the male penguin to sit on the eggs, clutching them tightly between their legs and their downy stomachs.

With the eggs covered like this, the penguins can still move from place to place although they look extremely odd when they do so.

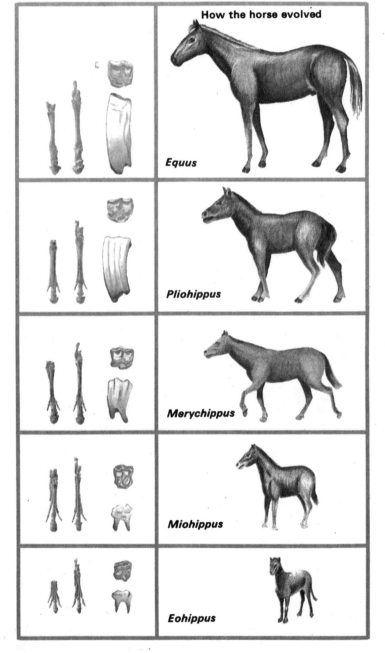

How the horse evolved

Equus

Pliohippus

Merychippus

Miohippus

Eohippus

When the female is sitting on the eggs, the male bird feeds her. He continues to do so for a time after the young birds are hatched.

There are seventeen species of penguins. They vary in height from 40 centimetres to more than a metre. They all live in the southern hemisphere and go on long migratory swims to escape severely cold weather.

How the praying mantis tricks its victims

The mantis can often be mistaken for a grasshopper but more careful observation will reveal that this creature is very different from that harmless insect.

The mantis has a soft, green colour which makes it difficult to see in the undergrowth. To trick its victims the mantis stands up straight and perfectly still, looking like a blade of grass. It holds its front legs with their powerful claws up in front of itself as if it were saying its prayers. This stance has won it the name of praying mantis although one of its American names, Devil's horse, might be more appropriate, for this is a ferocious insect. If any small creature comes too close, the mantis's front limbs suddenly spring forward and seize the victim which is dead within seconds.

How animals further the advance of science

To establish how effective a drug is it must be tested carefully and accurately and its effect on a living organism meticulously studied and noted. This is the task of pharmacology, a science which has made tremendous advances in less than a century.

The work of pharmacologists is often related to biochemistry, since they study the effects of

Praying mantis

Colony of Adélie penguins

foreign substances on cells or chemical systems of the body; and to psychiatry, for they also study the effects of drugs on the brain and behaviour.

The most significant stage in the discovery of a new drug is when the active substance that has curative properties is isolated. These substances are then checked for the effect they have on living tissues. This could be dangerous on a human being and even the curative properties of any drug can prove fatal if they are administered in wrong doses.

To overcome these difficulties scientists carry out their experiments on animals such as dogs, cats, mice, guinea pigs, rabbits and monkeys. Many such animals are sacrificed daily in the laboratories of the world, although most countries have strict laws which forbid the infliction of unnecessary pain on them.

One of the most common experiments is to infect these animals with germs to develop diseases. Sometimes various organs are removed from these laboratory animals for detailed study of their functions.

How plankton is formed in the sea

The surface of the seas and oceans is inhabited by hundreds of millions of tiny animals that are almost invisible to the naked eye. These little creatures float about in the ocean currents; their bodies are transparent and most of them can be seen properly only through a microscope. They are known as plankton and they provide many fish and other sea-animals with food.

The movement of plankton in the seas and oceans is very important because these small animals are always followed by shoals of fish. When herrings migrate by the million, they do so to follow the plankton which is about the only food the herring eats. The amount and distribution of plankton can effect the success or failure of a fishery.

Plankton can be gathered from the sea with special fine-mesh nets which were formerly made of silk but today are produced mainly of man-made fibres. On closer examination it is seen to be composed of animals and plants. The plankton comes under two main groups: macro plankton is large enough for the individual pieces to be seen with the naked eye; microplankton is microscopic. Some scientists also include a third category known as mesoplankton which comes somewhere between the two other groups in terms of size.

Microplankton contains many tiny algae. These are plants which reproduce themselves by simply splitting up. Macroplankton consists mainly of a vast range of tiny crustaceans which form the only food of whales. Microplankton also includes the larvae, or young, of crabs, crayfish, molluscs, starfish or the roe or eggs of large fish such as the tuna.

The algae also carry out the important task of putting oxygen into the sea water in the same way as plants do on dry land.

Plankton grows and multiplies at a tumultuous rate. It provides an abundant source of food for both fish that swim near the surface and those that live in the depths. This is because the plankton drifts down into the oceans when the animals of which it is composed die.

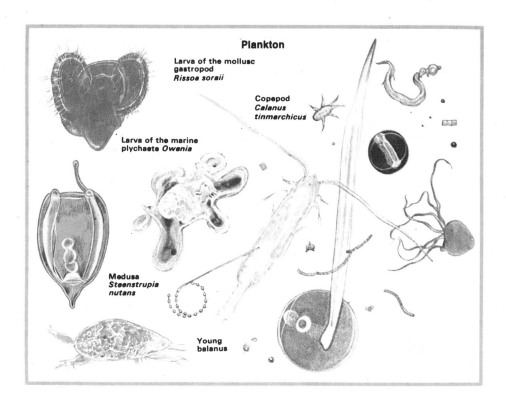

Plankton

Larva of the mollusc gastropod *Rissoa soraii*

Copepod *Calanus tinmarchicus*

Larva of the marine plychaete *Owenia*

Medusa *Steenstrupia nutans*

Young balanus

How the ant-eater feeds

The body of the ant-eater is covered in long hair that prevents ants from reaching its skin. For this reason it has no cause to fear insect bites when it tears the homes of ants apart with its strong claws.

The ant-eater makes its meal by shooting out its long, sticky, worm-like tongue and scooping up the ants that swarm all over the ground after their home has been destroyed. It has highly developed salivary glands which secrete the sticky substance that coats its tongue and traps the insects.

Giant ant-eater

How the squirrel flies

The American flying squirrel is one of the most unusual and beautiful of these animals. It is a nocturnal creature with large eyes, and feeds mainly on berries, seeds, nuts and insects. It does not have the thick, bushy tail of European squirrels, but it has a special fold of skin down both sides of its body.

When the flying squirrel leaps from tree to tree this fold of skin spreads out between its front and rear legs to form a sort of parachute which enables the animal to glide over quite long distances, sometimes covering more than 65 metres in a glide. The squirrel's flat tail acts as a sort of rudder.

There are also other varieties of flying squirrel in Africa and tropical parts of Asia. The best-known of these include the flying phalanger and the African scaly-tailed squirrel.

How bees produce wax and honey

The wax produced by bees is used in making honeycombs consisting of six-sided cells into each of which the queen bee lays an egg that will eventually give birth to an insect. Other cells in the honeycomb act as storage places for honey.

Bees produce wax in very thin sheets from eight glands on their abdomens. It takes some 1,250 of these sheets to make up one gramme of wax. We can imagine the amount of hard work that goes into the construction of a honeycomb. Not only does the bee produce the wax, but it also shapes it into the hexagonal cell.

The honey is nectar from flowers which has been gathered, concentrated and digested by the bees. The honey still has the scent of the flowers where the bees first found it.

How the queen bee lives in her hive

The queen bee is an extremely fertile animal. This insect is no more than 2 centimetres long but lays an average of 2,500 eggs a day at the rate of two eggs every minute. It does this throughout its entire life, accumulating a total of 2 million eggs.

Each egg is placed inside a hexagonal cell. If the larvae, as the infant bees are called, are fed on a substance known as royal jelly, they too, become queens. If they are just fed on pollen they grow into ordinary bees. But a beehive can contain only one queen. So the first queen bee to emerge from the cells kills all her potential rivals still in their cells and drives the old queen out. The old queen leaves with a swarm of bees still loyal to her to start another hive elsewhere.

Once the new queen begins her reign she carries out what is called her nuptial flight. As she flies through the air she is accompanied by male bees known as drones. The queen bee flies higher and higher and only the strongest of the drones can catch her and mate with her. The queen bee returns from her nuptial flight fertilized and sets to laying eggs assisted by a group of bees who feed her and look after all her needs.

How the prehistoric winged lizards flew

Perhaps we shall never know why reptiles should suddenly try to fly at a certain time in the history of the Earth. One thing is certain: in the rock layers formed about 130 million years ago, scientists have found the remains of many winged reptiles lying next to the bones of

Bees:
a) worker,
b) drone,
c) queen,
d) cell of the queen

dinosaurs. The first to leave fossilized remains behind were the pterosaurs. The front limbs of these reptiles ended in a sort of hand with a highly developed fourth finger. Along the sides of their bodies they had a fold of skin, rather like the membrane of a bat's wing, which was joined on to the front legs at the fourth finger to form a primitive wing.

These reptiles avoided moving about on the ground because the rough terrain could seriously damage their rather delicate wings. They spent most of their time gliding in the skies, and rested perched on rocks or trees so that they could launch themselves into flight again. If they fell on flat ground they had great difficulty in getting back into the air, for if they beat their wings too much they risked damaging them. So these winged reptiles would scramble up to some higher position on rocks, using their front limbs to climb with.

One of the earliest of the winged reptiles was the *Dimorphodon*. It looked like a monster bat and it was a large creature: its skull alone was about 22 centimetres long. Its mouth was lined with teeth that were large at the front and smaller at the back of the beak. The beak itself had a large pouch at the throat, rather like a pelican, and in this the reptile stored insects which it gathered during its flights. The *Dimorphodon* had powerful rear limbs which indicate it was a bird of prey.

How the female hornbill is imprisoned while she hatches the eggs

Like the toucan, the hornbill has an extremely large beak, but the two birds must not be confused. The hornbill's beak is different because it continues above the bird's head to form a sort of knob that looks like a helmet.

The male hornbill which feeds its 'im prisoned' mate

There are forty-five different species of hornbills, with loud, croaking voices and flapping wings. Their strong beaks can break the shells of the hardest

**Male and female
spiders of the genus
*Nephila***

nuts, but hornbills will also eat insects and small animals.

Most hornbills build their nests in a hollow tree. The male bird imprisons the female inside her nest by walling her in with dried mud while she hatches the eggs and cares for the young until they can fly. He leaves a small slit in the mud wall and through this he feeds his mate during the whole period she is sitting on the eggs.

How the lobster carries its eggs

Lobsters live along rocky coastlines of the Mediterranean and north Atlantic. They are crustaceans and related to shrimps, prawns and crabs. Like the shrimps, the female lobsters carry their eggs stuck to their abdomens for about ten months until they hatch. The eggs cling to the mother's body by means of a sticky substance and the animal also protects them by covering them with her fan-shaped tail.

The lobster has ten jointed legs, including two with strong claws. The spiny lobster has no large claws but uses its prickly limbs to defend itself.

The main food of lobsters is fish, alive or dead, and the invertebrates which live at the bottom of the sea. They also occasionally eat sea plants.

Lobsters look like prehistoric monsters that should have died out millions of years ago. They are not dangerous to man and because they are delicious to eat, they are the basis of important fisheries. Usually they are caught in quite shallow water by the use of lobster pots, creels or frames covered with netting.

How walruses use their tusks

The tusks of a walrus can grow to a length of almost 70 centimetres and are much sought after by ivory hunters. Walruses use their tusks for several purposes; as a weapon in their fierce battles to win a wife against rivals; to help them climb up rocks and ice when they come ashore; and to dig up clams from the seabed. These tusks are therefore very valuable to the animal but they are, in a sense, also its ruin.

One reason why walruses are not so numerous today and are confined to a few regions in the northern Pacific and the Atlantic, is that, since the ninth century A.D., hunters have slaughtered them for their ivory tusks. The Pacific walrus has longer, more slender tusks.

It was among the Eskimos of the arctic and subarctic regions that the art of carving ivory was most highly developed. Even the most everyday objects, such as harpoon heads, needle cases and the toggles for the dog harness, were decorated.

Walruses

How the bee-eater makes its strange nest

The nests of bee-eaters are strange constructions, like those of the fishing martin. The bee-eater uses its long beak to dig out deep tunnels on the steep banks of rivers. The tunnels open on to a room under the ground, which is the bird's nest. The floor of the nest is covered in butterflies' wings and the remains of insects.

These remains do not make a very comfortable bed but the young bee-eaters seem to like it.

The bee-eater is a tireless flier. From morning until night it goes in search of insects. While other birds help farmers by eating up grubs that live on plants, the bee-eater prefers to catch its victims as they fly along.

The only damage this bird does in hunting is to kill many bees and this angers bee-keepers.

The bee-eater with its brilliant plumage and pointed wings is related to the kingfisher. It is found in Europe and Australia.

Merops rubicus
or bee-eater, so called because its food includes bees and wasps

How spiders use their venom

There are about 40,000 species of spiders and nearly all of them have poison glands. Fortunately, in most cases the venom is very weak and has little or no effect on man. The bite of the tarantula was once thought to cause a disease called tarantism when the victim wept and danced wildly. Now it is known that the bite is not dangerous to man.

A few spiders, however, can injure people. One of these is the black widow which lives in North America. Its bite can cause intense pain, severe illness and even death, though this is rare.

In actual fact the mouth of a spider is made in such a way that it cannot really bite. These animals use their venom as a chemical to paralyze their victim. Scientists have found that the venom of spiders in some species breaks down the tissues of the victim and turns them into a sort of jelly which the spider then sucks up because it has no means of chewing its food.

If a spider is not hungry it does not kill its victim immediately. Instead, it imprisons it by wrapping a thick web of threads round it, waiting for the right moment to inject its venom.

Lampropelma, a genus of giant spider also mistakenly known as the tarantula

39

How the cuttlefish swims

Cuttlefish swim slowly along the sea bed, delicately exploring the sands with their two writhing tentacles which they use to catch their victims.

Like all cephalopods (from the Greek meaning 'feet attached to the head'), these fish have their heads surrounded by eight little arms fitted with suckers. They move through the water rather like jet aeroplanes, by shooting water through a special funnel.

Cuttlefish are about 15 centimetres long. The body consists of a bag which has a fin down either side. The cuttlefish has the amazing ability of changing colour according to its surroundings. Its skin has cells that contain pigments, or dyes, which the animal uses to blend in with its background. For this reason it is also known as the sea chameleon.

Sepia is obtained from the ink sacs of cuttlefish and is used as drawing ink and as a watercolour.

Cuttlefish are eaten in many countries. They form an important fishery in China and large numbers are tinned in Spain and Portugal. They have also been eaten since early times in Greece and Italy.

How a snail sees

The common snail is not a large animal but its ancestors were among the first living creatures on the Earth. One of the features of this mollusc is the set of four horns that protrude from its head rather like a set of periscopes. As soon as these horns are touched the snail pulls them in and they disappear from sight. These horns are the sense organs of the snail which enable it to feel and taste objects as well as to smell them.

In each of the two front feelers there is a small dark point that can go up and down inside the channel in which it is located. These are the eyes which the snail can pull back right into its head whenever there is danger about.

How snake's poison works

The real masters of venom are snakes. Man has come to know them ever since he first appeared on the Earth and has learned to hate and fear them. It is a hatred and fear that takes in all slithering crawling creatures, even if they are quite harmless.

The instinct that makes us shun these animals is a wise one for in many parts of the world there are a large number of dangerous and venomous snakes. Their venom varies from species to species and acts in many different ways: some snake venom can act on the nervous system; some can act on the blood, making it thicken or go thinner. Usually the effect of snake venom is rapid and leads to partial or total paralysis of the body. Death is usually caused by asphyxia.

In snakes the venom is a kind of saliva which often runs through special fangs that have a hollow passage in them. There are some snakes which do not have venom

Snail

fangs but their bite is still poisonous. The only poisonous snake in Europe is the viper, also known as the adder, of which there are many varieties.

Snakes vary considerably in size, from the small Syrian thread snake to the tropical pythons which can grow to a length of 10 metres.

How some sea-fish use their poison

There are certain fish which present serious dangers even to man because of their strength and ferocity. The shark is an obvious example, but among the most dangerous are the poisonous fish which use their venom in a number of ways.

Some have their flesh completely impregnated in poison and any attacker who bites them or eats them will die. Other fish impregnate their eggs with poison to protect their unborn young.

There are also fish with spines or fins that contain poison and others with teeth that carry venom, just like snakes.

The most unusual weapon belongs to the stingray. This is a strange, flat fish that spends much of its time on sandy or muddy bottoms of shallow waters where it is almost invisible. Most stingrays inhabit warm seas, but a few kinds are found in the rivers of South America.

If the fish is trodden on it lifts its tail which contains a long, poisonous sting that is usually kept in a sheath. This sting can inflict serious wounds, especially when the long, thin tail is lashed. The poison is painful; it can paralyze and, in some cases, prove fatal.

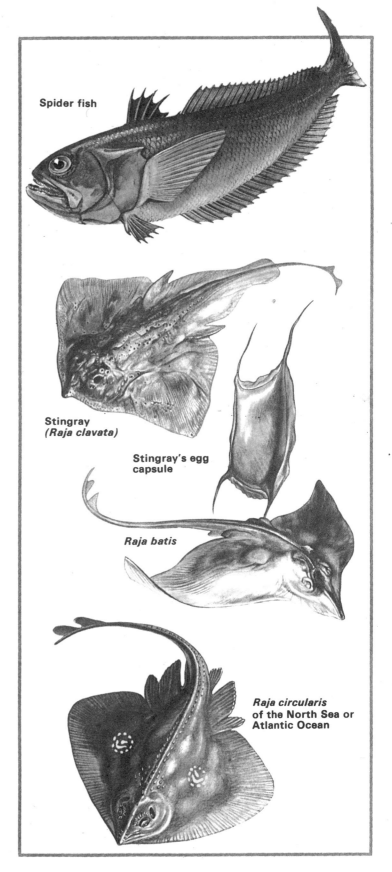

Spider fish

Stingray
(Raja clavata)

Stingray's egg capsule

Raja batis

Raja circularis
of the North Sea or
Atlantic Ocean

How the giraffe obtains its food

The most striking feature of the giraffe is its very long neck which gives this animal a lofty view of the world around it. Such a long neck has both its advantages and disadvantages. The advantages are that the giraffe can feed on the tasty, tender leaves which grow high up on the trees where no other animal can reach them. The long neck is also useful because the giraffe can look out over the savanna and see any danger from afar. One disadvantage is the difficulty the giraffe has in touching the ground with its head; every time it drinks it has to spread out its front legs in a rather awkward manner to bend down.

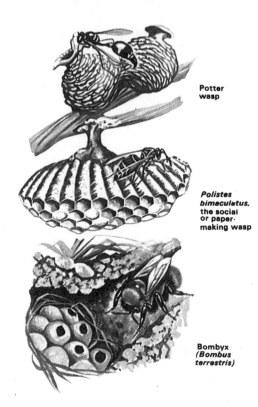

Potter wasp

Polistes bimaculatus, the social or paper-making wasp

Bombyx (Bombus terrestris)

How wasps catch crickets

Crickets dig their burrows with the openings towards the Sun but carefully concealed in the grass. On sunny days crickets love to sit by these openings and enjoy the sunshine whenever they are not looking for something to eat.

The wasp is the cricket's most feared enemy. Wasps often come down suddenly and without warning when the cricket is sunning itself. After a brief struggle the wasp usually succeeds in overcoming the cricket which it then paralyzes with several blows of its sting.

Once the cricket is paralyzed the wasp uses its little hooked claws to drag its victim back to its nest where the cricket will become a valuable source of food for the whole community of wasps.

How gnus behave when danger is near

Gnus are mammals that live mostly in central and southern Africa, grazing on the grasses and low scrub of the open plains. At one time there were many herds of them. They are very sociable animals and often mingle with herds of zebras, ostriches or antelopes.

Whenever strange intruders appear the gnus behave in a rather odd manner. They ruffle up their fur, paw the ground and go into a thundering charge. But after going only a short distance they stop, wheel round and see what effect their display is having. If the charge has made no impression then the gnu beats a hasty retreat. However the thundering sound of hooves of a charging herd of gnus is often enough to drive away any intending attacker.

The gnu is a ruminant and a very strongly-built animal. In South Africa it is kept on farms like a domestic beast. Its body resembles that of a horse but its head is very large and covered in a thick tuft of hair. It has a pair of sharply curving horns which are very thick at the base.

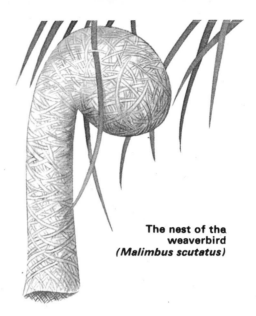

The nest of the weaverbird
(*Malimbus scutatus*)

usually a big acacia tree, several metres above the ground. The nest is shaped like a sharply pointed roof, has a very wide base and the surface is sloped to allow rainwater to drain away.

Underneath the edge of this roof which is thatched with dry grasses, there are the holes which are the entrances to the various private nests where the young weavers are hatched.

Sometimes an extremely large number of birds work together to build a nest that is so large it looks like a hut for humans from a distance.

How the sociable weaver builds its nest

The sociable weaver of south-western Africa gets its name from building giant communal nests together with other birds of its species.

These nests are like small cities sometimes inhabited by hundreds of birds. Each bird has its own private apartment in the nest city.

The sociable weavers' nests are built round the trunk of a tree,

About 300 weaverbirds can co-operate in building an enormous communal nest

THE HOW OF THE EARTH

How wind and rain can make pyramids

Erosion is a constant natural process by which rocks are worn away. This process is effected by the amount of rainfall and the strength and direction of the wind.

Sometimes the effects of erosion are so weird and wonderful it seems as if a magician has been at work. Some of the strangest effects can be seen in pyramids which resemble a series of pinnacles each surmounted by a rock.

These pyramids are the result of the softer underlying material being worn away while the harder rock at the top remains. The hard rocks act as an umbrella and protect the soil underneath from the attacks of rainfall. These rocks mark the former level of the ground before it was worn away by erosion.

The most famous of these formations include those in Monument Valley in Utah in the United States.

Various coral structures

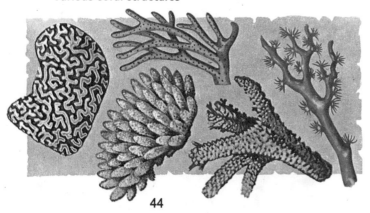

How coral forms in the sea

At first sight coral looks like some fossilized plant. But coral is the 'skeleton' of a mass of small animals known as polyps. The polyps emerge from their coral structure, waving their little tentacles to catch scraps of food. They look like small white blobs and have delicate whiskers on the ends of their tentacles which they use as fingers to take the food they catch to their mouths. The polyps are always ready to slip back into their coral shelter at the slightest sign of danger.

How lava goes hard

Lava is one of the substances that a volcano produces when it erupts. It consists of a material called magma which is a molten rock that rises from the depths of the Earth. The temperature of molten lava reaching the Earth's surface ranges from about 700° to 1,200°C. Most lava is thin and fast-moving and can spread out to great distances.

When the volcano has stopped erupting and the lava has been exposed to the air, it begins to cool, becoming hard and rocky on the outside while remaining soft and even liquid inside. If the sides of the volcano are steep the bottom layers of lava run off while the upper sections go hard. This process causes what is known as a lava tunnel.

Soil which began its life as lava is extremely fertile. For this reason people have always lived near volcanoes despite the danger of periodic eruptions and the risks involved.

How to recognize a glacial valley

When a glacier moves through a valley it exerts a tremendous force on the hillsides. The friction, or rubbing, of the ice mass is also increased by the large number of rocks which are frozen fast inside it and which act as abrasive or scouring elements. The glacier therefore scoops out great masses of soil and rock. When it has retreated or melted the marks of the rubbing or abrasion can be seen on the rocks. These rocks have rounded tops and are known as *roches moutonnées*, which means 'rocks shaped like sheep'. These rocks show heavy scratches known as striae, caused by the rubbing force of the glacier.

Glacial valleys can also be recognized in another way. In a river valley the flow of water is concentrated at one part of the valley's floor, so that a river valley is V-shaped. In a glacial valley the glacier is spread out all over the valley floor and a glacial valley is U-shaped.

Examples of glacial valleys include the fjords, the long sea inlets, of Norway. The sea now fills these long narrow bays but at one time they were completely locked in ice.

To the north of glacial valleys where the great glaciers are formed as a result of the accumulation of snow, there are cirques. These are vast hollows scooped out of the side of hills or mountains by ice and snow when they melt and fall away. In Scotland cirques are known as corries and in Wales as cwms. Sometimes two cirques are formed together and separated only by a narrow ridge called an arête.

A typical mountain of Chile

How rocky walls of mountains crumble

Rain, wind, frost and ice are the tools that nature uses to make even the largest mountains gradu-

Columnar basalt in the Auvergne, France

ally crumble down. This process is known as erosion and takes millions of years to complete its work. Some of the erosion results from the chemical decay of rocks caused by various substances in the atmosphere, and can be seen, for example, in the flaking of basalt. When this happens the rain breaks up the rock even more and washes it away.

The atmosphere also has a physical effect on rocks. Changes in the air temperature is one such effect. Rocks expand in heat, as any solid does, and contract or shrink in cold. This constant expansion and contraction eventually helps to crumble the rock.

Another physical force is the continual freezing and thawing of ice. This is a powerful factor because the water often freezes after running deep into the rock through a crack. The ice then acts from within the rock to break it up.

How hot mineral springs are formed

One of the best-known effects of the great heat that lies inside the Earth can be seen in hot, mineral springs that gush out of the surface of the Earth. These are rich in minerals such as common salt, which gives rise to 'bitter springs', and iron, sulphur and magnesia, giving medicinal waters.

Scientists differ in their opinions on how these hot springs began. Some believe they come straight up from underneath the ground where they were trapped millions of years ago during earth movements. Other scientists think the water began as rain which seeped through the soil, became heated and then rose again.

Perhaps both opinions are correct. It is certain, however, that the waters of these springs have flowed under the soil, become enriched with mineral salts and been heated to boiling point.

How fertile farm soil is formed

Air contains certain chemical substances which are present in greater quantities when the atmosphere is moist. These chemicals attack even the hardest rocks. To see how rocks can be affected one only needs to pick up a pebble from the sea or a river. On the outside the pebble is smooth and rounded: this is the result of the work of water and the air's chemical action. The inside of the pebble is still rough because it has not been reached by the external forces.

The chemical action of the atmosphere is extremely important. It can break down rocks and put oxygen into them by oxidation. The result is farm soil without which we cannot grow our food.

However, we must not think that agricultural soil is merely a collection of tiny particles of rock which have been crumbled away. Such a mixture does not contain many of the ingredients necessary to sustain plant life, and only certain primitive plants, such as lichens, can obtain any nourishment from it.

Soil becomes fertile when these pioneer' plants like lichens die and decay. Their decomposed bodies enrich the soil with their chemical substances to form a material known as humus. It is this humus, which is a mass of dead and decaying vegetation, which makes soil fertile.

How rapids are formed

Rapids in a river are a waterfall that has reached its old age. They are the remains of what was once a vertical fall of water such as the

Foz de Iguacu Falls, Paraguay

Niagara Falls. After millions of years the waterfall has worn the cliff away to a sloping bed of rocks.

The water still flows rapidly and tumbles about over the broken surface of the stream. It is dangerous to boats, sometimes making it completely impossible to sail up a river. But rapids are very useful in helping to produce electric power.

Shooting the rapids in canoes or kayaks is a popular sport in America and is also one of the events of the Olympic Games. At the Munich Games in 1972, a long stretch of artificial rapids was built specially for this sporting event.

How the solar system moves in space

During the 1700s after a great deal of hard work astronomers were able to calculate the speed and direction of many stars. By 1805 the astronomer Herschel proved that the Sun itself was subject to the same laws of movement. We now know that the Sun with its whole accompaniment of planets travels through space at the terrifying speed of about 270 kilometres a second together with the whole galaxy in which the solar system lies. The Sun also travels along a path of its own which is directed at a point in the heavens near the star Vega.

Herschel had studied the distant nebulae which astronomers before him believed to be millions of stars. Even the Milky Way was a nebula, but it was much brighter than the others and therefore must be nearer.

Herschel then thought that the Sun, like hundreds of other stars visible from the Earth, was part of a huge nebula, separate from all the others and forming a universe of its own: the galaxy.

During the 1870s the first powerful telescopes found other nebulae outside the galaxy and this proved that Herschel was right. New searches were made in our own century with the installation of the Mount Wilson telescope in 1905 and the one at Mount Palomar in 1948.

Today we can even begin to draw a map of the galaxy. It appears to be shaped like a flattened ball with a diameter of 100,000 light years (one light year is equal to 10 million million kilometres) and contains about 100,000 million stars.

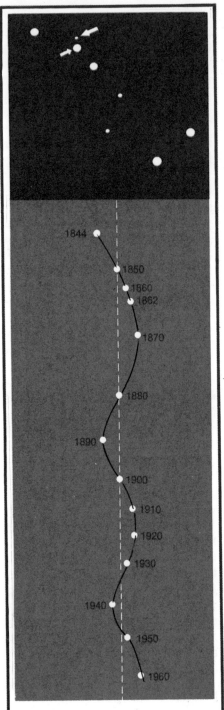

Above: position of Mizar and Alcor in Ursa Major

Below: the irregularities in the time of the movement of Sirius indicate the presence of a companion star

How double stars were discovered

There is a star in the constellation of Perseus which is called Algol. Every fifty-nine hours this star loses a great deal of its light and remains dimmed for about ten hours. Then it returns to its former brightness. The astonishing regularity with which Algol repeats this performance helped astronomers to solve the mystery the

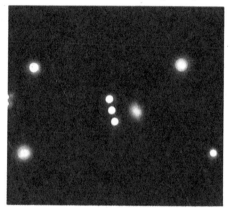

The multiple star Orionis known as Trapezius

star presented. Algol had been considered to be a single star but was discovered to be a double star. One of these stars was less bright and revolved round another, brighter, heavenly body. When the less bright star lies between us and the brighter body there is an eclipse.

Algol is a star system, one of many in the heavens. There are other star systems which have two, three, four or even six stars, as in Castor, in the constellation Gemini. Astronomers believe that one in three stars that can be seen with the naked eye are not really single stars, as they appear to be, but stellar systems composed of several stars. To discover such stellar systems requires complicated calculations and highly developed precision equipment.

How the inside of the Earth is made

Man has been able to explore the atmosphere around him and has even landed on the Moon and yet he still knows so little about the planet on which he lives. What he does know is confined to the surface or the crust: anything concerning the regions beneath the crust comes from deductions, suppositions and calculations. The

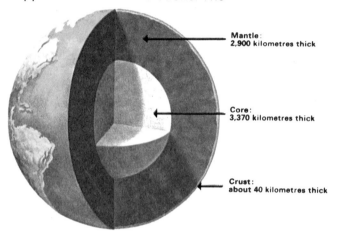

Mantle:
2,900 kilometres thick

Core:
3,370 kilometres thick

Crust:
about 40 kilometres thick

distance to the centre of our planet is about 6,371 kilometres. The deepest man has penetrated is about 12 kilometres in a geological exploration shaft.

We know that the central nucleus or core of the Earth is composed of heavy materials in a viscous or semi-molten state, and is at a constant high temperature. We have no idea of what fantastic temperatures may be reached at the centre of the Earth. We do know that lava, which rises from depths of up to 100 kilometres, is 1,000°C which is ten times the boiling point of water. Scientists who have measured the temperature of the Earth in non-volcanic areas have discovered that it rises by an average of one degree Centigrade for every 30 to 40 metres downwards.

How artificial satellites are used

Today there are many artificial satellites that revolve round the Earth. Why is all the time, money and effort required to launch them considered worthwhile? The answer is that the satellite performs many useful scientific tasks as it journeys through space.

Artificial satellites can act as spies that seek out military installations and equipment on the Earth below. Another function is to relay television and telephone communications between distant points of the globe.

They can study the solar radiation and environment of space and this knowledge helps us to understand the forces at work on our own planet and the causes of natural phenomena which effect our living conditions.

Meteorological satellites also exist which record details of weather conditions throughout the world and help in weather forecasting.

Various layers of rock each laid down at different times and each containing fossils of different reptiles

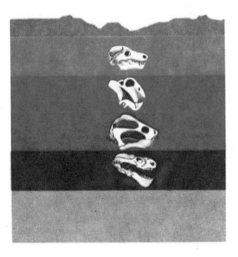

How we can discover the ancient history of the Earth

Geologists can read the history of the Earth in its rocks. From rocks it is possible to tell whether one area of the Earth is older than another and also in what age of the Earth's history a particular rock was formed.

There are three basic ways of studying rocks in order to obtain useful information relating to the Earth.

Firstly, the mineral content of the rock. This indicates the physical conditions in which the rock was formed and the age of the rock as compared with another. If, for example, one rock contains fragments of another rock, the fragments must be the older of the two.

Secondly, the fossilized remains found in certain rocks. The presence of fossils in a rock can tell us the sort of place where the rock was formed (the sea, a lake etc.). These fossils also indicate the age of the rock because we know that certain animals lived until a particular era in the Earth's history and then became extinct. The fossils can also give us an idea of the climate and weather conditions when the rock was formed.

Thirdly, the order of the rock layers or strata can reveal how a certain type of landscape was formed.

As a result of studying rocks closely geologists have learned that various types of landscape share common features throughout the world. They have also learned that rocks occur in certain major strata, each of which corresponds to a specific period in the history of the formation of the Earth as we know it today.

How fossils were formed

To understand the process that produces a fossil we can examine the trilobite.

This was a marine creature that lived on the sea bottom where it crawled along in search of food. At a certain point in time a part of the sea where it lived suddenly became laden with a huge mass of soil brought by rivers in flood. This muddy deposit buried millions of trilobites and for tens of millions of years the muddy deposits continued to build up on the ocean floor until they became huge underwater mountains.

The enormous weight of the mud caused the mountain to become as hard as rock. Then a great earth movement shook the area: the sea retreated and the mountain became dry land. Later still, other earth movements split the mountain apart to reveal the various layers of rock.

All this time the trilobite lay caught in the rock, its own body

Trilobite

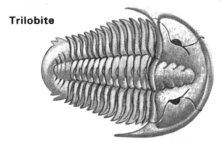

turned to stone. Then ice, wind and rain made the mountain crumble and one of the pieces slid down to the valley with the fossil of a trilobite inside it.

This is how the remains of these animals that once lived in the sea can be found now, many millions of years later, many kilometres inland.

Trilobites provide the best and most numerous fossils of the Cambrian Period, some 550 million years ago.

How the Earth was at the dawn of life

In the early part of the Palaeozoic Era, when the trilobite flourished, animal and plant life began to thrive and multiply in the oceans. The land regions, however, remained desolate and dead.

Not one blade of grass grew on the mountainside or the plains. Not one insect buzzed through the air which was mostly dark with heavy, rain-laden clouds. All was silence and solitude and there was no sign at all that one day the land regions would be inhabited. And not only inhabited, but covered in a mantle of green vegetation sheltering animals and life in general.

Before all this happened the Earth must have looked a terrible place: as bleak and lonely as the Moon landscape photographed by the astronauts in our own time.

Artist's impression of the surface of Mars

How an animal becomes fossilized

Men have been attracted to fossils since the earliest times. Even today we read with great interest any report about the discovery of the skeleton of some prehistoric animal.

The question arises: how can the fragile bones of any animal have stayed preserved for such a long time?

Much depends on the type of soil in which the bones came to rest. If the soil was damp and with a strong acid content, then the bones would not have lasted for very long: the chemicals in the soil would soon have broken them up into a powder.

But a damp soil with no harsh chemicals in it, often acts as a preservative. In this kind of soil the bones are gradually petrified, which means they are turned into stone.

When soil is moist and acid and completely without air, then even the soft tissues of an animal can be preserved through a process similar to mummification.

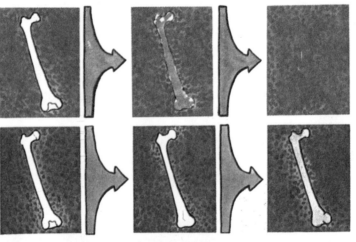

Acid-moist soil: matter disappears

Alkaline-moist soil: complete fossilization

Alkaline-dry soil: partial fossilization

Acid-moist soil with no air: soft tissues also preserved

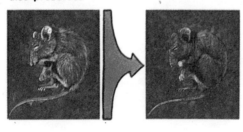

How the Earth's internal heat is used

The internal heat of the Earth is seen on the surface of the planet in volcanic activity. These manifestations of heat include *soffioni*, an Italian word to describe a hole in the earth through which jets of hot steam or unpleasant-smelling gases shoot out. These blow-holes are a sign of volcanic activity under the ground and the gases they release into the air come from molten rocks known as magma which lie at depths of between 5,000 and 6,000 metres.

Scientists found boric acid in these vents and an industry to extract this chemical substance was founded in Italy in 1818. Later it was discovered that the power of these gas jets could be harnessed for other tasks, including the production of electrical power, and the first geothermal electricity was generated

at Landarello, in Italy, in 1904.

There are four kinds of geothermal power: dry steam, as at Landarello; hot water, as at Reykjavik, in Iceland, where it is used to heat most of the city; low temperature areas in basins of sedimentary rock, containing water between 40 and 100°C which is used for agricultural purposes such as heating glasshouses; and high pressure zones found by petroleum drilling deep in sedimentary basins.

How life is possible in underground caves

Many strange animals live in the gloom of underground caves. Some of them were completely unknown until relatively recently when the science of speleology developed.

Speleology is the scientific study of caves from all points of view. These include, amongst other things, the discovery and exploration of caves; the study of their geological and chemical problems; and a study of their animal life.

It is difficult to imagine how any living creature could exist in these conditions but despite this there are many cave-dwelling animals under the ground. Most of them are tiny animals which, because of the lack of light, have no positive colour. They are either very pale or even transparent.

Since there is no plant life in the caves they live in, these little animals live on the flesh of other animals.

How underground rivers are formed

When rainwater which contains a certain amount of acid falls on limestone rocks, a strange process can take place. The limestone begins to break up and caverns, some of them enormous, start to form under the ground.

Such a terrain is known as karst. This term was first applied to the Carso, a limestone area along the Dalmation coast of Yugoslavia, but is now used to describe any area with these features.

Karst represents a limestone rock which is honeycombed with tunnels and caves through which the rainwater runs, seeking a way out. As the water moves along it wears away more and more of the surrounding rock to produce long tunnels which turn into underground rivers. These rivers eventually reach the sea after appearing at the surface in places.

Speleologists have tried to follow the course of some underground rivers but many passages are too narrow for a man to get through.

One way of following their course is to place dye in their waters whenever they appear at the surface. They can then be recognized when they break through again.

How stalactites and stalagmites are formed

Even people in ancient days knew that the constant dripping of water could wear away the hardest rock. Geologists have since discovered that these little drops of water not only wear away rocks but form others just as hard. It takes hundreds of thousands of drops of water to wear away one millimetre of stone; but it takes millions of drops to build up the same amount.

To see water which has turned into stone one has to go into a karstic cave. The first striking sight is of stalactites and stalagmites, stone pillars that descend from the ceiling or rise from the floor. Then there is the spectacular draped effect of the rock on the ceiling and walls of the cave. All these wonders have been created by dripping water. Each drop of water contains a microscopic piece of calcium: through the constant dripping these tiny specks of calcium have turned into rock pillars of dazzling beauty.

How a glacier is formed

Snow that falls on low ground does not lie for long and soon melts away in the first warmth of early spring. On higher ground snow remains for a longer time but even there it is usually all

melted away by May. But there are places where even the summer sunshine cannot banish the snow. This is on mountains like the Alps at heights of more than 3,000 metres.

This height is known to geographers as the snowline or the limit of persistent snow. It varies

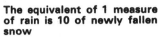
The equivalent of 1 measure of rain is 10 of newly fallen snow

The level of permanent snow varies with the latitude

Height in metres

4,500

3,000

1,500

Mt. Kilimanjaro 3°S

Mt. Blanc 46°N

Mt. Erebus 78°S

according to location on the globe: in the tropics, for example, the snowline is much higher, at about 5,500 metres, and in the polar regions it is practically at sea-level.

If all the snow that falls on the Earth were to stay on the ground winter after winter, all the highest mountain-tops would be covered many times over. But snow only stays on valleys and hollowed-out mountainsides to form snow-fields.

When snow falls it is light and feathery. A piece of snow of this type measuring a cubic metre weighs about 75 kilogrammes. But as the snow heaps up on the ground its weight causes the bottom layers to freeze into a hard glassy mass and the weight of a cubic metre rises to about 900 kilogrammes. The upper slopes of all the world's mountain ranges are covered in these masses of snow. Once it finds an outlet this frozen snow begins to move slowly like a gigantic river of ice and a glacier is born.

How weather forecasts are made

It was already known in the last century that when the barometer showed a low air pressure bad weather could be expected and when the arrow pointed to a high pressure good weather was on the way. When all the air pressures of a region are known a map can be drawn up to show them. On these maps are drawn lines to join places which have the same air pressure: these lines are called isobars. When all these lines are drawn they reveal various systems of air pressures.

The anticyclones are areas of high pressure which usually bring good weather. Cyclones, or depressions, are low-pressure areas and usually bring rainy or stormy weather.

Today meteorologists use equipment of great accuracy to probe the atmosphere around with a precision that would have seemed unbelievable not many years ago.

A copper axe moulded in stone

How man began to use metals

Man may well have discovered the existence of metals by accident. Perhaps one night as he warmed himself by the fire he noticed some of the stones round it begin to melt and flow into a red hot stream. Such a happening would have amazed him. But just as surprising must have been the fact that when this liquid fire cooled it had become hard. It was probably in this way that man first came to produce small quantities of copper, tin and iron

and a new era in human progress was born.

Very few metals are found in a pure state in nature: they are usually mixed with other elements. One of the strangest metals is mercury which has an extremely low melting point: it takes a temperature of −39°C to make mercury solidify.

There are metals which are lighter than water and can float in it like pieces of wood or cork. Lithium is one of these metals and its specific gravity is just over half that of water (0·534). It is, in fact, the lightest of all solid elements. Lithium is a white metal with a silvery lustre that quickly tarnishes when exposed to moist air, but it is soft and can only be used as an alloy with lead or aluminium.

Lithium was discovered comparatively recently. It was first isolated in Sweden in 1817 from a mineral known as petalite. The world's major producers of lithium in order of production are Russia, China, Zimbabwe, the United States and Brazil.

Ships fitted with meteorological equipment and posted at various fixed weather points report daily on weather conditions in their vicinities

How hail and frost are fought

Today's methods of dealing with hailstorms were first put forward 400 years ago by the Italian poet Giangiorgio Trissino who lived in Vicenza. His proposal was: 'We could prevent hailstorms from harming the Vicentino by placing cannons on certain mountain tops where clouds bearing hailstones usually gather. As soon as these clouds are seen the cannons should be fired into them to break them up and scatter them so that their hail will not fall . . .

This idea seemed very strange at the time, but it was not far from the truth for today aircraft can fly into clouds that are likely to produce hailstones and release large quantities of small crystals. The crystals may then either act to prevent the hailstones forming in the cloud or they may reduce the size of the hailstones so that they either melt to form raindrops as they fall to the ground or, if they do reach the ground, are too small to cause much damage.

Ice and frost can be fought by lighting large fires. It is not the heat of the fires that prevents the ice and frost forming, but the layer of smoke that lies over the ground and insulates it like a blanket from the cold air above. Scientists have also developed an artificial fog to do this.

How the modern science of meteorology was born

On 14 November 1854, a terrible storm erupted over the Black Sea, then the scene of the Crimean War. The British and French fleets met the full fury of the storm. After the tempest had died away two ships had sunk. The event caused much alarm. The question was asked: was it not possible to be prepared for such sudden bouts of bad weather and take precautions in advance?

The French scientist Urbain J. J. Leverrier then asked all European weather observers for information regarding wind speed, cloud formation and atmospheric disturbances which had been observed from 12 to 16 November. Using this information as a basis for his calculations, Leverrier was able to conclude that this storm had crossed the entire continent of Europe from west to east. If the weather observers had passed news of the storm on by telegraph its full force could have been avoided.

It was an idea and a few years later, on 1 December 1863, an atmospheric disturbance observed in Ireland was communicated to ports on the Atlantic coast of France and on the Mediterranean. When the storm arrived all shipping had taken cover and great damage was avoided. Meteorology had carried out its first service to mankind.

stratosphere

tropopause

troposphere

57

Stratocumulus

Nimbostratus

Cumulus

Cumulonimbus

Stratus

Altocumulus castellanus

How clouds form

The moisture in the air is the result of the evaporation of water by the heat of the Sun. The amount of evaporation depends on the quantity of water and the intensity of the Sun's heat. Another factor that contributes to the increase of atmospheric moisture is the breathing of living creatures.

All these factors combine to produce enormous quantities of water vapour which are continuously rising from the surface of the land and the sea and condensing in the atmosphere. When this happens the vapour turns into clouds of various types.

It was not until 1803 that clouds began to be classified scientifically. Luke Howard published a paper on clouds and the Latin terms which he used became the basis of the internationally accepted cloud classification. Further work was carried out towards the end of the century and the development of aviation stimulated further research.

Clouds have been classified into three main groups by international agreement. The classification depends on the height of the clouds above sea-level. The groups are: cirrus, cirrocumulus, cirrostratus, between 5,000 and 14,000 metres; altocumulus, altostratus, nimbostratus, between 2,000 and 7,000 metres; stratocumulus, stratus, below 2,000 metres. There are clouds that build up like pillars from the land into the sky to a height of over 6,000 metres. These include cumulus and cumulonimbus.

When the condensation of water vapour in the atmosphere goes beyond a certain limit, it turns into rain or snow.

Altostratus

Altocumulus

Cirrus

Cirrostratus

Cirrocumulus

How snow forms

When a cloud meets a very cold current of air, the tiny drops of water vapour that make up the cloud can suddenly turn into very thin pieces of ice. This can happen before these droplets have had time to condense into water, as occurs during rainfall.

In winter it is common for clouds in the sky to be full of minute pieces of ice instead of water vapour. These ice particles are tiny crystals that are long in shape and lighter than air so that they remain suspended in the air.

Snow falls when a certain number of factors are present. These are a combination of low air temperatures and air currents. The tiny particles of ice are then brought together; they become larger and heavier and fall as snowflakes.

When seen through a magnifying glass, snowflakes reveal a complicated and beautiful pattern based on a hexagon. Although snowflakes appear similar in size and structure there is a great variety in shape, size and pattern. It has even been said that no two snow crystals are the same.

How hail is formed

Much of the hail that falls on Europe occurs in summer though scientists believe it is caused by cold temperatures. Some meteorologists believe hail is formed when a current of hot air rises to about 1,000 to 2,000 metres and collides with a cold air current that is descending. The sudden lowering of the temperature in the warm air current freezes the moist air it contains into the little pellets of ice that form hail. This process

may be repeated several times, the hailstone gathering more and more coatings of ice, until it becomes heavy and falls.

Other meteorologists think that hail is produced by electrical processes.

Whatever the cause hail is a constant threat to farmers who for centuries have sought ways of defending their fields from it.

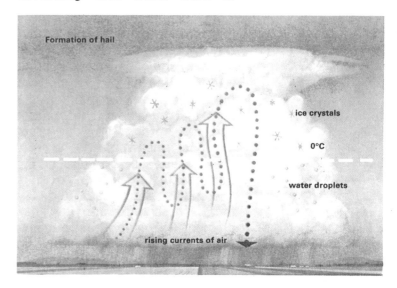

Formation of hail

ice crystals

0°C

water droplets

rising currents of air

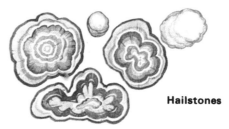

Hailstones

Hailstorms do not usually affect large areas, but they can be so concentrated and intense that they destroy an entire year's crop wherever they strike. Vineyards are frequently affected in this way.

Occasionally huge hailstorms can fall and cause enormous damage. In November 1889 hailstones the size of cricket balls fell in the streets of Louth in New South Wales.

British pottery of the Bronze Age

How clay deposits form

If we take some water from a river in full flow or from a pond, after a while certain particles will fall to the bottom of the glass or receptacle. These particles previously floated in the water giving it a brown, muddy colour.

We can imagine what this process would be like magnified many millions of times and occurring for long periods. This is how clay deposits gather.

Rocks and pebbles require quite a strong force to move them along, but the fine particles of clay are so light that they float in the water and are borne along for great distances in rivers to the sea. When these clay particles finally come to rest they form what is known as argillacious or clay rocks. These rocks are very fine-grained and smooth and many become soft if soaked in water.

Clays are basically made up of silicas, aluminium and water in various amounts together with other elements such as iron, calcium, chalk and mica. No other earth material has so many uses or such a wide importance. One of the purest forms of clay is kaolin which is used in making porcelain and china. Impure clays have been used for bricks, tiles and the crude types of pottery since the earliest times.

How precious stones are cut

The cutting and polishing of diamonds are very delicate operations that can be carried out only by skilled craftsmen who pass on their art from one generation to the next.

Not all diamonds can be cut and transformed into elegant stones. The more impure ones and fragments obtained from cutting gems are used in industry. Diamonds are extremely hard and are valuable in cutting or polishing the hardest of metallic alloys.

Another precious stone that is extremely rare and very valuable is the emerald which is a beautiful green colour. Emeralds are usually small. When one is larger than ten carats and free from impurities and faults it is much more valuable than a diamond of the same size.

Much of the value of these gems depends on the way they have been cut. The usual way is to cut surfaces or facets on them so that they will refract or break up the light that passes through the stone. The effect is to produce a number of small prisms which break up the light into the beautiful flashing colours of the rainbow. Great skill is necessary at every stage of diamond cutting, but especially during faceting, as the angles of the facets must be exact to give the maximum amount of brilliance and to preserve the

Spear-heads of the Bronze Age

symmetry of the stone.

The diagram on this page shows the various ways in which gem stones can be cut: (1) marquise; (2) drop or pendeloque; (3) briolette; (4a) rosecut, seen from above; (4b) rosecut seen from the side; (5a) flat cabochon, seen from the side; (5b) double cabochon, seen from the side; (6a) brilliant cut, seen from above; (6b) brilliant, seen from bottom; (6c) brilliant, side view; (7a) step cut, seen from above; (7b) step cut, seen from bottom; (7c) step cut, side view.

The upper part of the faceted gem is called the crown and the lower is called the base or pavilion.

How tunny fish is caught in the Mediterranean

The tunny fish is a large, active creature up to 3 metres long and sometimes weighing as much as 450 kilogrammes. It lives in both warm and temperate seas and has a body temperature well above that of the water in which it swims. During the mating season thousands of tunny fish gather together along the coast of Europe and America in the Atlantic Ocean or in the Mediterranean as far as the Black Sea.

In the Mediterranean fishermen use a very old method of catching tunny fish. This involves rigging a

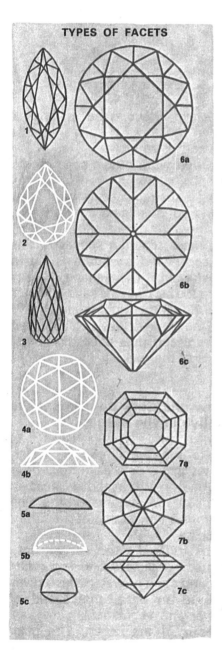

TYPES OF FACETS

Peridot crystals in their rock matrix

Cut peridot

Cut tourmalines

Tourmaline crystals

system of nets which forces the fish to swim into an enclosed space known as the death chamber.

When the fish have reached this place the nets are raised out of the water and the killing process, known as the *mattanza*, begins. The fish are killed with spears and harpoons and then hoisted on to waiting boats. It is a rather exhausting way of fishing but the catches are usually large and profitable, for tunny fish is very tasty and in one season more than 1,000 tons can be caught.

How the sand dunes of the desert are formed

Wind carries objects along as it blows over the surface of the ground, and the flatter and more arid the land underneath, the more effective the wind's action becomes. In the deserts, for example, the wind shifts enormous quantities of sand, raising it, grain by grain, and carrying it over great distances to form dunes. During desert storms some large dunes of sand can be moved by more than 10 metres.

In some cases sands from the Sahara desert have been carried by the wind to as far as northern Europe. In China there are large regions of soil which consists of fine particles that have been blown there by the wind.

Sand dunes are also found on sandy coasts with onshore winds and near rivers with sandy beds which are exposed during the dry season. Evidence of their existence is found in many geological periods.

As well as carrying sand along, the wind also breaks down and destroys. When sand and dust

are driven along in a strong wind against rocks, they act like sandpaper and wear away, little by little, the hard rocky areas that they strike. The destructive force

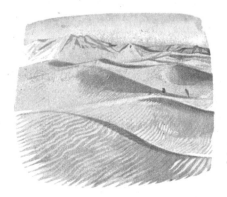

of wind-blown sand is greater when the rocks it strikes against are soft or crumbly.

Often wind-blown sand carves strange shapes in rocks, resembling abstract sculptures that stand up in isolated groups in the vastness of desert areas. One of the most common shapes of this type of wind sculpture is like a mushroom. This shape results from the fact that the sand particles that do all the rubbing are always in the lower levels of the air current and thus affect the lower parts of the rock.

How the date palm manages to live in the desert

There is a Bedouin saying which states that a date palm must have 'its feet in water and its head in the sun'. For this reason the date palm is a typical tree of the desert oases.

Its roots dig very deeply into the soil until they find an underground store of water which gives rise to an oasis, that island of water and vegetation in the vast wastes of the desert. The palm needs a great deal of sunshine to grow vigorously and this explains the second part of the Bedouin saying.

A fully grown date palm tree stands more than 20 metres high. It has a slender trunk with a tuft of leaves at the top. Under these leaves there grow clusters of flowers which produce the berries that we know as dates. They are red at first and then turn brown. They have a sweet flesh and contain only one seed. A single large branch of the tree may carry more than 1,000 dates weighing about 10 kilogrammes.

The date palm is very important in the life of desert people. This is not just because of its fruit but for every part of the tree. The wood from the trunk is used in building; the leaves are dried and make thatch roofs for huts as well as mats and ropes; the sap of the tree can be made into an alcoholic drink; and the seeds or stones of the date can be ground to make a beverage like coffee. Date sugar, which is produced in India, is obtained from the sap of the *Phoenix sylvestris*, which is closely related to the date palm.

Date palm
(genus *Phoenix*)

mud where it can live for months on end, especially if it goes deep enough to find an underground layer of water.

Lungfish are among the most ancient bony fishes and are very like those which lived 200 million years ago, at the beginning of the Mesozoic Era.

How fish can live in the desert

Although it is difficult to believe, there are fish living in the desert. Several important expeditions have gone to the Sahara to uncover the mystery of these fish which are sometimes found scores of metres down.

The most famous is the lungfish which lives in the larger African rivers. When these rivers overflow their waters can spread out to desert regions to form small lakes or ponds. When the lake dries up the lungfish buries itself in wet

Left: an African lungfish in its lair. Right: the Australian lungfish *Neocera-todus* (above) and *Protopterus africanus* (below)

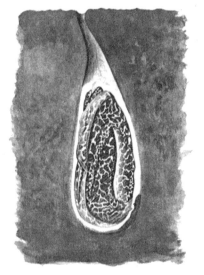

How new kinds of food are spread

The fight against hunger, or occasionally the desire to taste something new, has always urged man on in his quest for new foods which can be either plentiful and cheap or rare and expensive. For this reason rice, previously grown mainly in Asia, began to be grown on a large scale in Italy during the Middle Ages. It was brought back to Europe by the merchant-venturers of Venice and Pisa and the soldiers who took part in the Crusades.

The discovery of America opened up great opportunities for Europe in the way of food. In 1519

Almagro discovers Lake Poopo in Bolivia

Hernan Cortés seized the city of Mexico and found there a food market that was 'twice as large as the city of Salamanca' in Spain, according to the historian Diaz. This market was full of food that the Europeans had never seen before. The items included pancakes made of maize flour, turkeys,

potato pancakes and sweetmeats made of cocoa.

It took several hundred years before these strange new foods, like tomatoes and certain varieties of beans, spread to other parts of the world. Once they had been eaten and enjoyed they became a normal part of the everyday diet of people throughout the world, just as the potato did.

The tendency today is to go back to simple foods that are easy to digest.

How swordfish are caught in Sicily

Fishermen have hunted swordfish off the eastern coasts of Sicily for many hundreds of years. They use an extremely ancient method that never fails to attract large crowds of tourists to come to see it in operation.

The swordfish is a large animal, taking its name from the long, thin, spear-like part of its face that juts forward. It uses this bony spike as a weapon of offence to spear the large numbers of fish on which it lives. The sword fish can also turn its weapon on to any fisherman who tries to catch it.

The fishermen still use harpoons to catch swordfish. A sailor on the crow's nest of a ship spots the fish

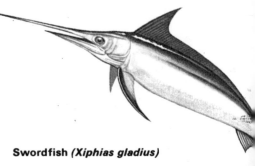

Swordfish (Xiphias gladius)

and shouts a warning. It takes tremendous skill and accuracy to hit a swordfish at its vital point and prevent it from charging against a fishing boat and endangering the crew.

Swordfish are often more than 3 metres long and can weigh more than 150 kilogrammes. Some zoologists believe this fish is the fastest swimmer in the sea. It relies on the powerful beating of its tail fin rather than the undulations of its body, as most fish do, and its stiff body glides rapidly and straight through the water.

How sea-fishing is carried out

Fishing is one of the oldest activities known to man. Early man who lived on houses erected on poles above the water of lakes, soon learned how to catch the silent creatures that swam around underneath the surrounding waters. The fishing methods of those primitive peoples did not differ much from the lines, nets and hooks of today.

The implements used in fishing can be quite complicated, such as the lobster pots that are sunk, laden with bait, to the sea-bed and the nets which are rigged up by groups of people working together. When these nets are dragged along the water they are known as trawls.

Other types of nets are placed in the water to form a ring which is then gradually closed round the fish and lifted out of the water. This method is known as purse seining.

In other netting systems fishermen simply block the fish's means of escape and force them to swim into a special area where they are caught.

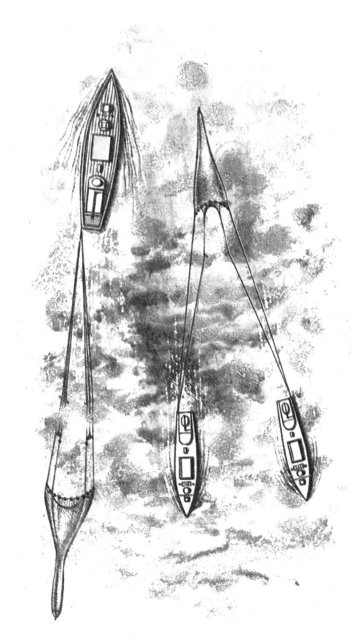

A trawler pulling its trawl net along through the water (left). Two trawlers pulling a single trawl to fish nearer the surface of the sea (right)

Shrimp and prawn fishing is carried out by boats using dragnets

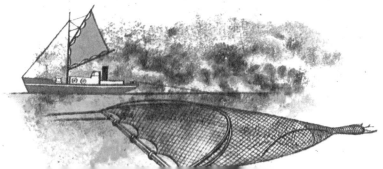

The old method of catching whales

How whales are hunted

Whales are not fish though they spend all their lives in the sea: they are mammals and the largest animals known to us. In order to breathe they have to rise to the surface of the sea every so often and that is when they are spotted.

Whale-hunting is a very ancient pursuit. Stone Age man probably hunted the smaller whales and dolphins, and the Eskimos and North American Indians whaled from early times. It requires very strong ships and skilled men who are tough enough to stand up to the hard life.

Until the 1900s whale-hunting was done by large sailing ships. These vessels launched smaller boats whenever a whale was sighted. The boats, manned by a crew of rowers and harpoonists, then went off in pursuit of their prey.

Today whales are hunted by small, fast ships. These vessels are very manoeuvrable and are equipped with a special gun that fires a harpoon. The harpoon contains an explosive charge and when it strikes the whale the animal dies almost instantly. In this way the old races between rowing boats and whales, which often ended in disaster for the sailors, are a thing of the past.

Large factory ships now process whales which have been caught, extracting their oil and other materials which are put to many uses.

Whaling on the scale made possible with explosive harpoons and factory ships has seriously depleted the number of whales, bringing several species to the point of extinction.

How methane gas deposits are formed

Methane is a colourless, odourless gas that comes from the decomposition of organic matter, including both farm and town refuse. Methane can also be produced chemically in a laboratory or extracted industrially from coke. But most of this gas is obtained from natural deposits which lie under the soil.

This type of methane is also the product of fermentation over a period of hundreds of millions of

A modern whaler and a harpoon gun

years. It originated from what was once a vast amount of small plant and animal life. These plants and animals became buried in mud and sand and through the ages hardened into rock.

The great forces at work in the bowels of the Earth, such as heat and pressure, then acted on these organic remains to change them into petroleum or natural gas.

Methane is lighter than air and is only slightly soluble in water. It burns readily in air with a pale, slightly luminous flame and is very hot. It is a stable material, but a mixture of methane and air can be highly explosive, as is shown by the explosions in coal mines.

How beet-sugar was first produced

The sugar-beet was known as a garden vegetable and for cattle fodder before it was valued for its sugar. As early as the 1500s, however, we come across the first accounts of the sweet juice obtained from boiling these plants.

It was not until the 1700s that the sugar-beet industry made its first simple beginnings. The idea came from a German scientist called Marggraf.

In 1747 he obtained 50 grammes of pure sugar by treating 200 grammes of dried root of beet with crude ethyl alcohol. Other scientists took up the experiments. Governments donated land and money for further research to be carried out and the first sugar-beet factory was built in Silesia in 1803.

Eventually, by the 1850s, beet sugar was able to compete with cane sugar. Today about a quarter of the world's sugar is produced from sugar-beet.

How maps are drawn

The ancient people had a very inaccurate idea of the size and shape of the Earth. They represented it in strange ways, imagining it was shaped like a flat disc surrounded by mysterious seas and oceans.

At one time it took a great deal of patient, detailed work to draw the map of a region. Today, cartography, as the art of map-drawing is called, is done very rapidly and with great accuracy.

Maps are now drawn by computers which can read photographs of regions taken from the air. All that is required is an aeroplane with a special camera on board to fly over the area to be charted and to take a series of photographs as it moves through the air. A greater number of maps are now produced than ever before, giving more diverse and accurate information.

A topographical map of the Canterbury region published by C. Packe in 1743

67

THE HOW OF SCIENCE AND TECHNOLOGY

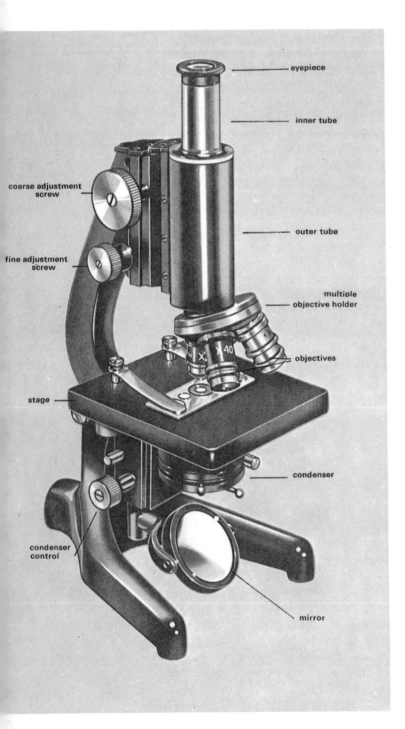

coarse adjustment screw

fine adjustment screw

stage

condenser control

eyepiece

inner tube

outer tube

multiple objective holder

objectives

condenser

mirror

How the microscope works

We do not know exactly when man first discovered that objects seemed much larger when seen through a specially shaped piece of glass. There are some very old stories but they are all vague. The known history of the microscope begins in the seventeenth century when the Dutchman, Anton van Leeuwenhoek, invented a simple microscope consisting of a single lens with a relatively high magnification. The first compound microscope was devised in 1590 by Zacharias Janssen.

The word microscope comes from the Greek *micros* meaning 'small' and *skopeein* meaning 'to look'. The instrument works with two lenses or discs of glass. The upper lens is the eyepiece and the lower one is the objective. The objective lens magnifies the object and the eyepiece lens enlarges the magnification. In modern instruments both the eyepiece and the objective consist of several lenses, so arranged that they rectify the distortion caused by the curvature of the glass.

The objects to be examined are placed on a glass slide. These objects are cut very thin so that light shines through them. In a microscope the light is reflected through the objects by a mirror. Scientists also use electronic microscopes which can magnify objects millions of times.

The basic parts of a microscope are the condenser which illuminates; the focusing mechanism operated by coarse or fine adjusting screws; and a variable diaphragm that controls the amount of light that goes into the condenser.

hunters' such as Koch, Pasteur, Bang, Schaudinn, Eberth, Loeffler and others. Microbes cause the body to produce a substance called antibodies which defend the body. These antibodies were first produced artifically in bodies through vaccination.

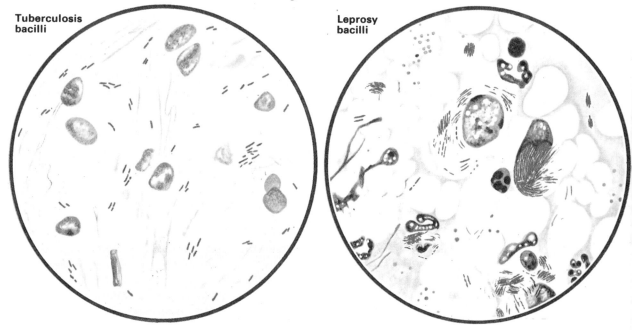

Tuberculosis bacilli

Leprosy bacilli

How disease microbes are fought

The victories of modern medicine are linked with the researches carried out by scientists into the causes of disease.

Microbes are tiny plants like microscopic fungi which enter our bodies in the air we breathe, with the food we eat and the drink we swallow. When they enter our bloodstream they can cause infection and make us ill. Every disease has a microbe as its cause. The microbe can sometimes pass from person to person causing the disease to spread.

Today we know how to cure many diseases and we owe it all to various famous 'germ

The first vaccination ever carried out was done by the British doctor, Edward Jenner (1749–1823), against smallpox. Jenner's experiment was a complete success. Later chemical substances were discovered to kill microbes. These included the arseno-benzoles of the German, Paul Ehrlich (1854–1915), and the sulphonamides of another German, Gerhard Domagk (1895–1964). But it was only during the Second World War that antibiotics were discovered. Two scientists played a leading role in finding these drugs. One was the British scientist, Sir Alexander Fleming, who discovered penicillin, and the other was the American, Selman Waksman, who discovered streptomycin.

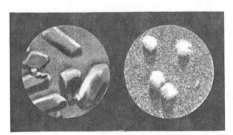

Crystals of the poliomyelitis virus (left) and of influenza (right)

How viruses are studied and fought

There exist in nature tiny little organisms which are much smaller than microbes. They are so small that they cannot be seen through an ordinary microscope and their existence came to light only through research carried out with electronic microscopes which can magnify objects millions of times.

These strange organisms, which are still little-known, were called filtrable viruses because they could pass through the very finest of 'nets' used by scientists to catch bacteria. They are parasitic, in that they multiply only in living cells. The diseases caused by viruses are known as viroses and they affect people, animals and plants.

It is extremely important to establish if a virus, when found, is pathogenic (causing disease) or non-pathogenic (harmless).

How the barometer was born and how it works

Even air has weight and, like any solid object, it presses down on the surface of the Earth. Scientists decided to measure the amount of this pressure and the Italian Galileo was the first to succeed. He used a very long tube, closed at one end, which he filled with water and then placed the open end in a receptacle full of water. The water in the tube fell, stopping at a height of 10 metres. A few years later, in 1643, a pupil of Galileo named Evangelista Torricelli carried out further experiments using a heavier liquid than water: mercury. The mercury rose inside its glass tube by 76 centimetres. The apparatus was given the name barometer from, the

Mercury barometer

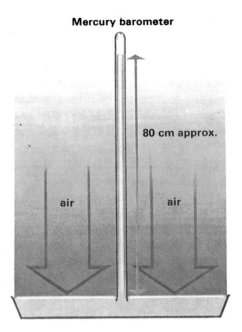

80 cm approx.

air   air

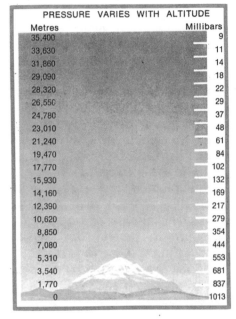

PRESSURE VARIES WITH ALTITUDE	
Metres	Millibars
35,400	9
33,630	11
31,860	14
29,090	18
28,320	22
26,550	29
24,780	37
23,010	48
21,240	61
19,470	84
17,770	102
15,930	132
14,160	169
12,390	217
10,620	279
8,850	354
7,080	444
5,310	553
3,540	681
1,770	837
0	1013

Greek *baros* meaning 'weight' and *metron* meaning 'measure'. Torricelli soon noticed that the height of the mercury column varied with changes in air pressure. About 1647 Blaise Pascal's experiments finally convinced people of the correctness of Torricelli's ideas.

The most modern form of this instrument is the aneroid barometer, from the Greek *a* meaning 'without' and *neros* meaning 'liquid'. The aneroid barometer consists of a small steel box which contains a vacuum. The pressure of the air outside the box can cause the surface of the box to move in or out. A needle on the dial records the movements of the box along a graduated scale to show the changes in air pressure.

This type of barometer is smaller and more portable than a mercury barometer but it is not quite as accurate. It has first to be calibrated or set to a mercury barometer before it can be used.

How the ancestor of today's bicycles was made

There were some vehicles using wheels and pedals in Europe in the middle of the eighteenth century, but the first machine that resembled a modern bicycle did not appear until 1790. In that year the Frenchman, the Comte de Sivrac, designed and built a rudimentary means of transport which he called the *vélocipède*.

This machine consisted of two wheels joined together by a piece of wood. The rider sat astride the machine and propelled it along by pushing first one foot and then the other along the ground. This machine became fairly successful in Paris during the bloody period of the Reign of Terror.

In 1818 the German Baron Karl von Drais modified the *vélocipède*. He introduced handle-bars to the machine and made the front wheel manoeuvrable. This machine was known as a hobby horse in Britain and as a *draisienne* on the Continent. It proved very successful throughout Europe.

Two British mechanics, Johnson and Knight, began to make these machines in iron and they proved lighter and more stable than in wood. The *vélocipède*, however, remained a strange toy until 1861 when the pedal to turn the wheel was invented. This development turned the machine into a true means of transport. Later refinements included the use of ball-bearings and the enlargement of the front wheel on which the pedals acted. This produced the well-known penny-farthing machine, *Ariel*, which was invented in 1871 in England by James Starley, the 'father of the cycle industry'.

The penny-farthing *Ariel* of 1871

How electrical power is transported

One of the great advantages of electricity is the ease with which it can be transported. All the same some major operations are necessary to carry, or transmit, electricity from one point to another. This involves machinery, cables and other equipment used in the generating industry.

The three main parts of the system are: the centres of production; the transmission system through which electrical power is carried from power stations to the main sub-stations which transform it from high to lower voltage; and the distribution system which takes electricity to every user.

Most modern systems use alternating current known as A.C. This is because it is simpler to vary its intensity and requires less complicated generators to produce.

Electrical systems must be as efficient as possible which means they must carry electricity without losing any of it on the way. The quantities of electricity carried today are very large and require high tension.

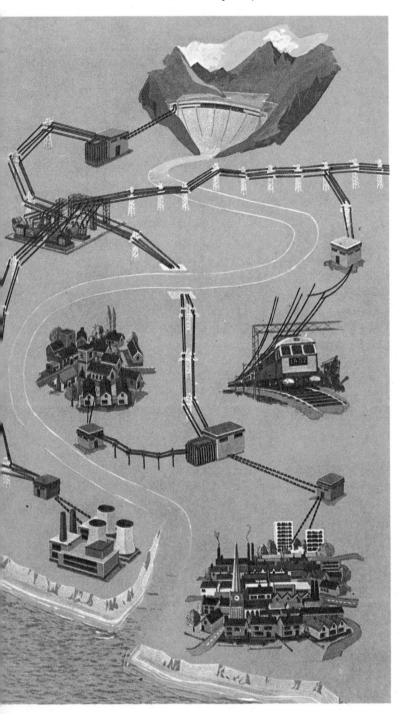

The highest tension used is 750 kilovolts, though 380 kilovolts is usually the peak in most countries. These high tensions create certain problems which have to be solved through better insulation of the current to prevent leaks or losses as it is being carried along the cables.

One type of power loss is known as the crown effect. It can be seen at night when a bluish haze glows round the high tension wires. Power losses can be considerable and lessen the power that eventually reaches the consumer at the receiving end of the system.

Most transmission lines have a tension ranging from 115 to 175 kilovolts. The tension in the distribution of electricity is lower ranging from 220 volts monophase to 400 volts three-phase. Electric power is supplied with a constant frequency except in the United States and in some regions of Japan where 60 Hz is used as a frequency. The world standard is 50 Hz.

To provide for emergencies duplicate circuits and apparatus

tried to travel along a bad conductor the latter would resist so much that it glowed until it became white-hot.

A carbon filament, for example, gave out a good deal of light; but the light did not last very long because the carbon would

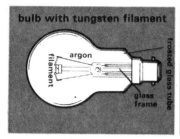

bulb with tungsten filament

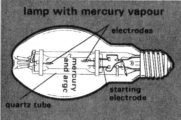

lamp with mercury vapour

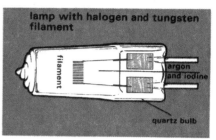

lamp with halogen and tungsten filament

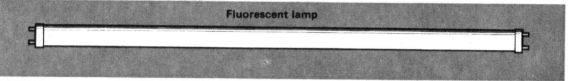

Fluorescent lamp

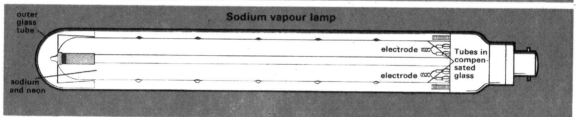

Sodium vapour lamp

are provided, resulting in many circuit arrangements or systems. At least two main transmission circuits are normally provided from a main generating station to each major sub-station, each capable of supplying the load for a time if the other is out of service.

How the electric light bulb was born

Thomas Edison had discovered in his experiments that there were certain bodies through which electric power flowed more easily. He called these good conductors and other bodies that resisted the flow of electric power he called bad conductors. When electricity

soon burn itself up as it was in contact with the oxygen in the air.

Edison then carried out an experiment inside a glass bulb from which he had removed all the air. This time the light of the glowing filament lasted much longer and the first electric light bulb was born.

Carbon filaments have now been replaced by tungsten wire as its high melting point, low rate of evaporation and low electrical consumption make it most suitable for use in light bulbs. A further improvement has been the introduction of an inert gas into the bulb. This was at first nitrogen but is now a mixture of 88 per cent argon and 12 per cent nitrogen.

Dornier Do 31

LTV-Hiller-Ryan XC-142A

Fairey Rotodyne

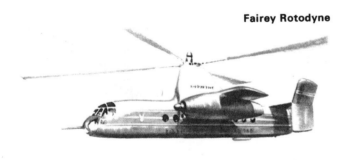

A Westland project for a tilt-wing VTOL airliner

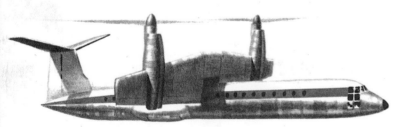

How some aeroplanes can take off vertically

Most aeroplanes take off horizontally from a specially built runway. A new chapter in the history of aviation began with the development of aeroplanes that could take off or land vertically. This first happened on 2 November 1954 when a small Convair aeroplane named the XFY-1 and nicknamed *Pogo,* rose straight into the air through the force produced by two propellers that measured almost 5 metres long. The two propellers rotated in opposite directions to each other and were driven by a turbine of 5,850 horse power.

The first study into vertical take-off began in the United States in 1920; but it took more than thirty years to solve the many problems surrounding the project.

An aeroplane that takes off or lands on the ground vertically, like a helicopter, is called a VTOL which are the initials of 'vertical take-off and landing'. Another VTOL that resembled the *Pogo* was the X-13, an American machine fitted with a jet turbine. The way in which a jet aeroplane can take off at a very steep angle with its nose high in the air is one of the by-products of research in this field.

Another means of obtaining VTOL flight was to develop variable jet outlets as was done on the *Kestrel.* Yet another method is to incline the source of the thrust, such as the rotors, propeller blades or engines, to the required angle. This is the method used in the German aeroplane VJ-101C and for the American X-19 and X-22A.

A fourth system is to move the wings of the aeroplane in an arc of 90° so that the engines exert vertical power. This is the system used in the American aeroplane XC-142.

One of the most successful VTOLs is the Hawker Siddeley Harrier which is in service with the U.S. Marines and the Royal Air Force. This aircraft works by diverting part of the thrust of its jet engine downwards at take-off and landing, providing as much lift as the Harrier pilot requires to manœuvre effectively.

How an aeroplane journey takes place

An air trip for most passengers begins with a coach journey to the airport. The passengers then board the aeroplane, walking up steps or along ramps that lead directly to the doors. When all the passengers are aboard the aeroplane, the doors are hermetically sealed. The aeroplane then travels slowly, or taxis, to the point of take-off. During the entire time the pilot is in constant radio contact with the control tower.

The staff in the control tower is responsible for all the air traffic of the airport. When an aeroplane approaches the airport the control tower tells it which route to take and what speed to travel at. The radio messages between the aeroplane and the control tower are all tape recorded.

On departure, the flight crew of an aeroplane are provided with all the information necessary to navigate the route to their destination. They may feed the information into the aeroplane's computer, which then controls the flight. The crew also check with air traffic controllers by radio as they pass various points.

When visibility is bad the aero-

New York, John
F. Kennedy Airport

plane is guided as it lands by an 'approach control' service that uses radar to show the pilot the way. Along the runways, which are usually hard-surfaced with concrete or asphalt, there are white lights and the end of the runway is marked by green lights. A line of blue lights shows the pilot the path he must follow after he has landed and red lights indicate obstacles and hazards to be avoided.

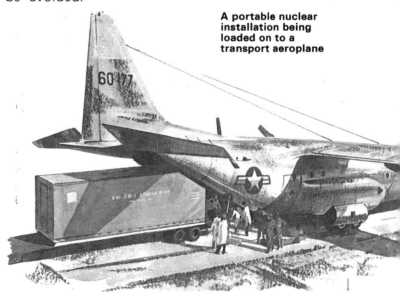

A portable nuclear installation being loaded on to a transport aeroplane

include spectacles with bifocal lenses and a stove that bore his name. His greatest achievement in the field of science, however, was the invention of the lightning conductor. The study of electricity received a great impetus during the 1700s. Franklin took part in these studies and set out to prove that a lightning flash was the discharge of electricity.

In 1752 he carried out his famous experiment in which he flew a silk kite with an iron point on it. Franklin used a metal wire to hoist the kite up into a thunderstorm. He wore silk gloves to protect himself. As the kite rose into the thunderclouds it was struck by a bolt of lightning. The electrical charge ran down the wire and into the ground. On the basis of this experiment the first lightning conductor was made.

How sound travels through the air

Everybody knows whether a sound is pleasant or unpleasant, loud or soft, mellow or sharp, but few people can actually explain what sound is and what are its qualities.

The string of a guitar or a harp is silent until it is plucked with the finger or a plectrum and set into vibration. The skin of a drum does not produce any sound until it is struck with a drumstick and made to vibrate. The sound of an accordion comes from the vibration of its reeds. The sound of the saxophone is also produced by the vibration of its reed. In a trumpet the noise comes from air that is thrust into the instrument and vibrated.

All sounds—the human voice, the noises made by animals, the tinkling of a bell or the buzzing of

How the lightning conductor was born

The lightning conductor, a highly useful invention, was the brainchild of the American, Benjamin Franklin (1706–90), Franklin was a brilliant man, being an economist, a writer, a politician, a philosopher, a printer and a scientist. He has been called 'the first civilized American' and the courage of his ideas earned him the name of 'the Voltaire of America'.

Franklin invented several objects that are now familiar. These

insects—is the result of vibration. Scientists have also discovered that there can be no sound if there is no air to be vibrated.

An experiment was once carried out in which a bell was placed inside a glass jar. As soon as all the air was removed from the jar the ringing of the bell could no longer be heard.

Astronauts have confirmed that there is absolute silence in space.

It is easy, therefore, to see that sound spreads through the atmosphere like waves or ripples that spread outwards in a pond when something drops into it.

The Vigilant anti-tank guided missile can pierce armour-plating 55 centimetres thick

How firearms were invented

The invention of gunpowder led naturally to the development of firearms, beginning with the cannon.

It meant the end of one era and the start of a new one. The gallant knight clad in his shining armour could now be felled by a humble little infantryman or foot soldier. Great turreted castles were no longer the safe and unassailable redoubts but could be knocked down with a heavy artillery barrage.

Early cannons were shaped like large pots which narrowed at the mouth and were often highly decorated with scrolls and inscriptions. They were about a metre long and placed on a stout wooden trestle. These cannons were charged with gunpowder and a huge ball-shaped projectile. The gunner would then set light to the gunpowder through a hole in the cannon and set off the explosion which projected the cannon ball.

These cannons were extremely heavy, clumsy and noisy and were inaccurate at all but very close range. They were dangerous not only to the enemy but also to the people who fired them, for sometimes they would explode with no warning, causing death and destruction. But they were a greatly feared weapon in the field of battle especially by the foot soldier.

How modern projectiles were developed

Until the middle of the nineteenth century the inside of the barrel of a cannon had no thread or rifling. It was quite smooth and the projectiles fired from cannons were simply round balls. They did not have a large range and were not very accurate: it was extremely difficult to hit a target with them at distances of more than 3,000 metres.

Projectiles could not be made too large for they would have needed cannons with enormously broad barrels. Then the idea occurred of making long projectiles which weighed more. The inside of the barrel of cannons was rifled with winding lines. When the projectile was fired it was twisted by these lines so that it came out of the cannon's mouth spinning rapidly but kept in a straight line. Because of its shape the projectile, or shell, travelled farther and was more accurate.

How ultrasonics are produced and used

The human ear can perceive sounds within the range of 16 and 16,000 vibrations a second and in some exceptional cases the upper limit can be as high as 20,000 vibrations. Ultrasonics lie beyond these limits: they are sound waves which have certain unexpected qualities. Long before man discovered the existence of this range of sound, nature had endowed many animals with the power of either emitting ultrasonic noises or hearing them as moths can hear the ultrasonic sounds produced by bats. Insects, for example, by moving the ringed segments of their bodies, or rubbing their legs against their hard body shells or fluttering their wings, produce ultrasonic sound with which they can communicate with one another over appreciable distances.

There are various pieces of apparatus to produce ultrasonic sound. They all work on the principle of the siren or the whistle: that is, they produce vibrations in a current of air that is subjected to high pressure.

In generators that operate on a magnetodynamic or magnetostrictive principle, it is an electric magnet that produces the energy. In piezoelectric generators the principle is based on the characteristics of certain crystals.

The use of ultrasonics covers a very broad field, including the food industry, mechanics, medicine and botany. The effectiveness of these mysterious sound waves lies in their power of penetrating solid, liquid or gaseous bodies by acting on their microscopic particles. Ultrasonic sound at high power produces cavitation, the formation of tiny holes, in a liquid. This is useful in the production of alloys and emulsions, and in cleaning processes and milk sterilization. Another use of ultrasonics is sonar, an echo-location process that detects underwater objects and finds the depth of water beneath a vessel. At low power, ultrasound is used in a similar way to examine internal organs and unborn babies.

How the refracting telescope is made

The telescope does not magnify objects but brings them nearer by using the principle of refraction through two or more lenses.

In the refracting telescope the first lens is placed at the wide end of the telescope and is convex in shape. This is called the objective lens, which brings the image closer but turns it upside down.

The light rays from this image reach the second lens which is known as the eyepiece lens. In Galileo's telescope this was concave, but in 1611 Kepler suggested a convex eyepiece and this came into general use in the middle of the seventeenth century. The shape of the eyepiece lens refracts or pushes back the light rays so that the image now turns the right way up.

The power of a telescope depends on the curvature of its lenses. To focus the instrument the objective lens and the eyepiece lens must be moved in relation to each other. For this reason a telescope is made of two or more tubular sections which can slide within one another. In binoculars the focus is worked through a knurled nut which is turned.

How railway traffic is directed

When the first railways began to operate it was suggested that a messenger should ride on a horse ahead of the train to tell people of its approach and warn the engine driver of any obstacles along the track.

Soon the train was able to travel much faster than the horse. Men with flags stood beside the track and either signalled the train-driver to stop or waved him on.

The problem of travel safety grew as trains increased in speed and numbers and level crossings with gates were built as well as viaducts to take trains over dangerous or difficult places.

Eventually a comprehensive system of mechanical signalling was evolved. Semaphore signals that swung up or down on a tall pole beside the track were the most common. Nowadays the majority of large railway stations have colour-light signals, with red meaning 'stop', green 'go' and amber 'caution'.

All these signals are now worked electrically. It is no longer necessary for a man with a watch to check the various times when trains pass, open gates or decide which track the train will go on to and make a note of trains which have been delayed. Today all these tasks are done by computers and the signal posts of large stations are completely automated.

New signalling station at Osnabrück, West Germany

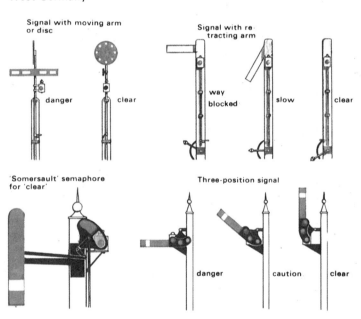

Inside a central signalling post where an illuminated plan of the track shows the position of every train

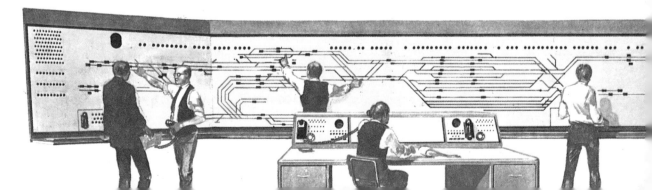

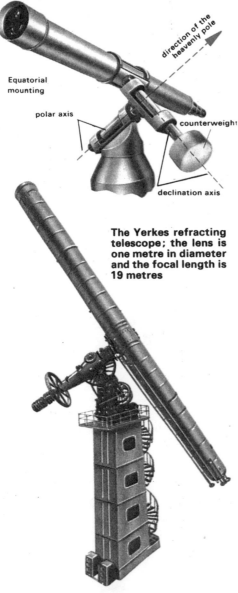

The Hale reflector at Mount Palomar with a diameter of 5·08 metres

Equatorial mounting

polar axis

direction of the heavenly pole

counterweight

declination axis

The Yerkes refracting telescope; the lens is one metre in diameter and the focal length is 19 metres

How reflecting telescopes are made

The first optical instruments with which the heavens were explored were large telescopes similar to the one first developed in Holland in 1608 and perfected by Galileo.

It was Sir Isaac Newton who replaced the lenses with mirrors. A large concave mirror placed at the foot of the tube reflects a portion of the sky and magnifies it. A second mirror receives this image and projects it to the eye. The wider the concave mirror, the brighter the image.

Today, the world's largest mirror telescope is at Zelenchukskaya in the Caucasus Mountains in Russia. The main mirror is 6 metres in diameter. It weighs 70 tonnes and it took 16 years to build the telescope.

Such a large telescope is equipped with complicated machinery to manoeuvre it with precision. The telescope is placed inside a large dome which can revolve on special tracks. This allows it to scan the entire sky. The magnification, or the apparent increase in the size of the object examined, depends on the distance that can be regulated between the mirror and the focus. The luminosity, or brightness, of the image depends on the energy emitted by the image which is increased by the size of the mirror. The objects brought into focus can be photographed or observed directly.

The radiotelescope is completely different and is used in radioastronomy. These huge, delicate instruments consist basically of an antenna, or aerial, that picks up radio waves produced by the Sun, the stars or the galaxy. One of the best known examples is at Jodrell Bank.

How a camera works

A camera is a fairly simple piece of equipment in its basic structure. One must not be put off by the numerous levers, buttons, scales and other gadgets on the outside. These are all extremely useful aids but are not completely essential.

The essential part of the machine is what gives it its name: the camera obscura. This is Latin for dark room. Photographs are produced when rays of light penetrate into this dark chamber. The light must enter through a small opening and strike against a sensitive film. The surface of the film is covered in an emulsion of chemicals which capture the images being carried by the light rays. The small opening, or aperture, must have a mechanism to cover it to stop light from entering all the time. The mechanism must also be able to open the aperture to let the light in. This mechanism is called the shutter. In a simple camera this is about the only moving part.

In more expensive cameras the fittings include mechanisms which can vary the exposure time which determines how long the shutter will stay open. This can range from a thousandth of a second for fast-moving subjects to one second or more for still dimly-lit scenes. Other controls include an aperture selector to vary the amount of light passing through the lens, and a focusing mechanism to produce a sharp image.

The camera obscura has long been known to man and Leonardo da Vinci made accurate drawings of it in the fifteenth century. It was not until 1839, however, that the first commercially available cameras were made in Paris by Alphonse Giroux for Daguerre.

How motion pictures were invented

In 1831 the Belgian physicist Joseph Plateau produced an apparatus which he called the phenakistoscope. This was followed by other devices such as the zoetrope or 'wheel of life' of the British inventor William Horner in 1834 and the praxinoscope of the Frenchman Emile Reynaud in 1880. Despite their difficult names these apparatuses were all fairly simple and they all exploited a certain characteristic of the human eye.

If an object is placed before our eye its image is picked up by the retina, an extremely sensitive screen inside the eyeball. Every change of object outside causes a change in the image received by the retina and if the changes are rapid enough a whole line of images can blend into one.

In the phenakistoscope and the other machines a series of images showing the various stages of a person in movement were shown on a revolving drum. All the images ran together and the viewer received the impression of continuous movement. Modern animated cartoons are also produced by a rapid succession of drawings.

An important development in motion pictures took place in 1889 when the famous American

A magic lantern of the nineteenth century

inventor, Thomas Edison, succeeded in using photographs instead of drawings. The photographs were taken one after the other on one roll of film. Edison then invented the kinetoscope to show his moving pictures. This was a kind of peep-show device which showed viewers about fifteen seconds of life-like movement.

The first truly modern cinematographic machine was produced in 1895. In that year the brothers Auguste and Louis Lumière of France patented their famous and historic 'cinematograph'.

How the lens of a camera is adjusted

The lens of a camera is placed in front of the small aperture or opening that lets light into the dark chamber, known as the camera obscura.

The more perfected the lens, the sharper and more accurate will be the photograph produced; the wider the lens, the greater the amount of light that will enter the camera. In this way, to photograph an object in poor light the ideal lens should be as wide as possible; to photograph an object in brilliant sunshine only a very small lens aperture is needed.

That is why the camera is fitted with a mechanism to adjust the aperture of the lens. The mechanism consists of a diaphragm that works just like the iris of a human eye: when the light is bright the hole in the diaphragm is small and when the light is poor the hole is made large.

There is an adjustment scale on cameras that gives various degrees of apertures. This is known as the f scale. On the f scale the lower the number the wider the aperture.

Therefore an aperture of f 2.8 is usually the widest the iris of a camera will open. An aperture of f 16 or f 22 is the smallest iris opening.

In any reasonably well developed camera the aperture must be set and the time of the exposure fixed before a photograph is taken. These two operations depend on the amount of light around the object to be photographed.

Another factor to be regulated before taking a photograph is the distance between the camera and the subject. In a good camera the lens can be turned and set to various distances. These are shown on the edge of the lens in figures that represent distances in metres from close range up to 'infinity' for very distant objects.

How ice is produced in a refrigerator

It was far more difficult for man to discover how to produce artificial cold than it was for him to produce warmth.

In olden days man tried to keep things cool during the summer by using snow or ice. This was a very difficult process. The snow and ice had to be carried down from the high mountain tops and stored in specially built places.

The ancient Romans, for example, brought their snow and ice from the Apennine mountains. They dug large chambers in the ground which they called *officinae reponendae nivis*. This meant snow store. The store was covered in wooden boards and the ice was brought to the towns from the Apennine region near Rome and in Sicily from Mount Etna.

The first experiments to produce

ice artificially began in the seventeenth century. It was later discovered that in specified conditions certain substances changed from a solid into a liquid state. This fusion, or melting process, was found to be caused through the absorption of heat by those substances. As the heat was absorbed it was accompanied by a steady cooling of the temperature. Further experiments showed that the same absorption of heat could be carried out by evaporating any liquid. An example of this is when a sudden breeze evaporates the perspiration from our faces and makes us feel quite chilly.

It is on this principle of heat absorption that ordinary household refrigerators work. The most commonly used liquid to bring about cooling is ammonia gas in solution. This solution runs through coiled tubes. It starts as a liquid and through compression becomes a gas which absorbs the surrounding warmth. This process is repeated over and over again until ice begins to form.

The first household refrigerator was made early in the nineteenth century. Since 1918 their use has become more and more widespread.

How percussion instruments are made

Percussion instruments have developed greatly in modern times. The drum, which is the basic percussion instrument, used to be made by stretching a piece of animal skin across a framework. This skin, when struck with the hands or a solid object, produced sounds the loudness and softness of which could be controlled.

The large kettle drums used in symphony orchestras are called timpani. They consist of a bowl-shaped metal shell' over which calf skin is stretched. The tension of the skin, and so the pitch of the drum, can be varied by handscrews fixed to the shell, and by other mechanical devices, including a pedal. Other types of drum cannot be tuned and they merely produce sound. The *gran cassa* which is a bass drum, the cymbals, the gong, side drums and triangles add colour and atmosphere to music.

Other percussion instruments include the marimba and castanets. An interesting percussion instrument is the xylophone which consists of a series of wooden bars each producing its own note when struck with a hammer.

A nineteenth-century timpani

Modern timpani

African marimbas with keys and resonators

The *Times-Herald* racing car of F. Duryea, 1895

How the first motor cars were made

The word 'automobile', which is another way of saying motor car, means 'moving by itself'. The motor car travels without being pulled by a horse or any other animal and with no visible force to make its wheels go round. For a long time inventors and engineers wondered how such a machine could be produced. One of the first attempts to produce an automobile was made during the eighteenth century. It was a very ramshackle affair and can still be seen today in the National Museum in Paris. The machine was designed by the French engineer, Nicholas Joseph Cugnot.

Cugnot's idea was to exploit the steam engine invented by Watt and use it to power a vehicle. He drew up plans which he submitted to the War Ministry since the machine was meant to carry heavy artillery. Cugnot was authorized to make a prototype. The machine he produced was a large, heavy, steam-powered tricycle. His model of 1769 was said to have run for twenty minutes at just over 5 kilometres an hour while carrying four people. Cugnot then built a larger vehicle. During a test run at Vincennes the machine got out of control and crashed into a wall, demolishing it.

The accident gave ammunition to Cugnot's opponents and the experiments stopped. It took many more years before attempts were resumed to make a motor car.

How the internal combustion engine works

The combustion engine seems a complicated piece of machinery but it consists of the following basic parts: the cylinder, the piston, the connecting rod, the inlet and

The first Michelin tyres were tested on a Peugeot of 1895

The Obéissante of 1873

exhaust valves, the carburettor, the sparking plugs and the crankshaft.

A piston moves in each cylinder of the engine, performing an up-and-down motion. The motion of the piston is transmitted to the crankshaft by way of the connecting rod and then on to the other parts of the mechanism that turn the wheels.

The movement of the piston goes through four stages or strokes. The first stroke occurs as the piston moves down the cylinder and the inlet valve opens and admits a mixture of air and petrol vapour from the carburettor. The piston then rises and strongly compresses this mixture until it becomes explosive. At that point an electrical spark jumps from the plug and causes the mixture to ignite. The resulting explosion pushes the piston down again causing it to turn the crankshaft which then turns the wheels. When the piston moves back up the cylinder, the cylinder's exhaust valve opens and the burnt gases are expelled. This whole process is repeated thousands of times a minute in four basic strokes: induction, compression, power, exhaust.

How the internal combustion engine is lubricated and kept cool

The component parts of any engine must be lubricated or oiled regularly. Lubrication provides a film of oil which reduces the friction that would quickly destroy rubbing parts. The lubricant commonly used is refined from crude oil and is improved with additives that reduce oxidation and corrosion and act as cleaning agents.

In a motor car there is a basin, known as the sump, or oil pan, underneath the engine. This contains the oil which is pumped round the engine while it is running.

The internal combustion engine must also be kept relatively cool. This can be done with air or water. Air-cooling is produced by the pressurized inlet of air into the cooling fins of a cylinder and other parts designed to get rid of excess heat. Water-cooling is produced by water being pumped constantly round the engine from the radiator, which is kept cool by the airstream and by a fan which also works the water-pump.

In winter anti-freeze liquids are added to the engine's water jacket to prevent it from freezing and damaging the cylinder block.

How the differential works in a motor car

When a motor car goes round a corner or a bend the inside wheels have a shorter distance to travel than the outside wheels. For this reason the inside wheels have to travel more slowly than the outside ones. This difference in wheel speeds is made possible through the differential.

The differential is a mechanism that consists of an axle that joins two wheels, usually the rear ones. In the middle of the axle there is a round shell that contains a series of geared wheels including the crown wheel. The pinion, which is part of the propeller shaft that runs from the gear-box of the car, sets these geared wheels into motion. When the car turns a corner the geared wheels of the differential vary the speeds of the wheels until the car is on a straight path again and both rear wheels travelling at the same speed.

How a rocket works

You may have seen a certain type of lawn sprinkler which works by spinning round and round as the water squirts from it. The spinning movement is caused by the pressure of the water pushing against the movable arm of the sprinkler.

Sir Isaac Newton noticed something like this happening and it led him to discover an important law of nature. Newton's law was that for every action in one direction there is an equal action in an opposite direction. In the case of the lawn sprinkler the water goes in and pushes in one direction and the sprinkler turns in the opposite direction.

The same law explains why a rifle recoils sharply when it is fired. The firing of the gun is known as the action and the recoil of the gun is the reaction.

This principle is what makes rockets speed through the air. Rockets are fuelled by very highly compressed gases. When these gases are violently released from the tail of the rocket the reaction they set up gives the rocket a mighty push in the direction opposite to the gas flow.

The greater the distance to be travelled, the greater must be the initial thrust. When *Saturn V* was launched, for example, its five engines consumed kerosene and liquid-oxygen at a rate of 15 tons per second.

Saturn V

The rocket principle can be illustrated by a simple balloon

The missile leaving a Komar-class patrol boat

How radar works

We have all at one time or another heard the echo of our own voice. An echo is caused by sound waves being bounced back from a solid obstacle, rather like a rubber ball bouncing off a wall. The same thing happens to radio waves which are sent out by a powerful transmitter. When the waves collide with a solid object they bounce back and can be picked up by a receiving set which is usually located at the same place as the transmitter. Since the speed of these waves is known we can tell how far away the obstacle is by calculating how long the waves take to cover the distance. This is how radar works.

The word 'radar' is an abbreviated form of the name 'radio detection and ranging'. Radar is now used everywhere: at airports, missile bases, space centres for following and tracking satellites and on ships and aircraft for automatic navigation. A simple form of radar is used by police to detect speeding vehicles.

A battery of Sander rockets using solid fuel was used by Fritz von Opel, the German motor car engineer, to reach a speed of 152 kilometres an hour in a glider. In 1928 Opel reached a speed of 200 kilometres an hour using rockets in his experimental car *Rak 2*

The tail-first *Ente* sailplane which was the first rocket plane to fly successfully

How the value of vitamins was discovered

Vitamins are substances of mainly vegetable origin which provide an essential part of our food and nourishment. Lack of vitamins leads to ill health. The Australian aborigines have for many centuries treated certain eye diseases by applying the liver of a fish similar to the tuna to the affected part of the eye. Scientists discovered that the liver of this fish was rich in vitamin A which is excellent for eyesight.

A common disease in Asia is beriberi which causes paralysis and swelling throughout the body. In 1882 a doctor in the Japanese navy discovered that beriberi could be cured by eating barley instead of rice. This doctor had noticed that many Japanese sailors ate a lot of polished rice and they contracted a disease similar to beriberi. These sailors were the victims of a lack of vitamins found on the outer husk of a grain of rice.

In 1897, Dr. Eijkman, a doctor working in a prison in Java, found that chickens fed on polished rice contracted a disease that resembled beriberi. The chickens became better if they were fed with unpolished rice. Eijkman concluded that the outer part of a grain of rice contained a vitamin that fought beriberi. This was vitamin B. A lack of vitamin B caused beriberi and its use on a victim of this disease cured him.

The children who lived in the damp and unhealthy slums of London often suffered from rickets which weakens the bones and distorts their shape. In 1650 a certain Dr. Glisson found that cod liver oil benefited these children. The oil is rich in vitamin D which prevents rickets.

In 1936 two American scientists raised a sow on an artificial diet containing all the vitamins known at the time (A, B, C, D). The scientists also put another sow on the same diet but gave the second animal a large quantity of lettuce to eat. The first sow proved unable to bear even one piglet; the second sow produced a horde of youngsters. The two scientists concluded that the lettuce contained a hitherto unknown vitamin which they named E. Vitamin E is also known as the fertility vitamin. Other vitamins have since been discovered in other vegetables.

The pharmaceutical industry can produce many of these vitamins artificially.

Emperor apple

Granny Smith apple

How the salt is removed from sea-water

For years engineers and scientists have tried to solve the massive problem of removing salt from sea-water to meet the growing demand for fresh water. Several land-based stills have been built in arid regions such as Kuwait, where local oil deposits supply the fuel, but production costs are high.

Scientists have been able to desalinate sea-water by using nuclear power. The diagram on this page shows how such a de-salination plant works. Basically what happens is that the water is heated until it evaporates. The vapour is then condensed through cooling and distilled to produce fresh water. The only problem is to have a source of considerable heat which is cheap to use. Such heat could come from nuclear reactors.

How synthetic fibres were produced

As far back as 1665 a British scientist predicted that artificial fibres would one day be produced. The first experiments were carried out about 200 years later by a Swiss scientist in Lausanne and the first industrial production of the fibre took place in 1884 under the Frenchman Chardonnet.

Naturally it took some time for the fibres to become popular. In the first decades of the twentieth century rayon was being pro-duced from cellulose. Protein fib-res, made from such natural mate-rials as casein, in skimmed milk, peanuts and soya beans, were also produced.

Today, the production of syn-thetic resins has made artificial fibres into a vast industry. Its products include nylon, dralon, orlon and dacron which are used all over the world.

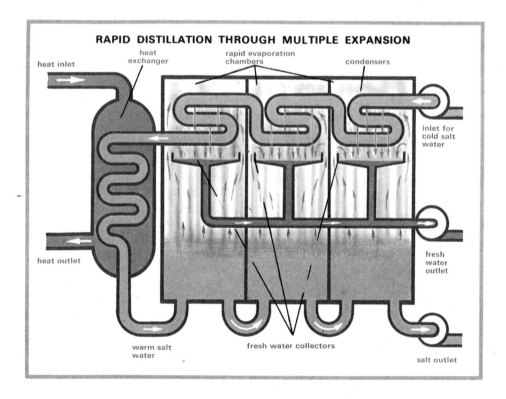

RAPID DISTILLATION THROUGH MULTIPLE EXPANSION

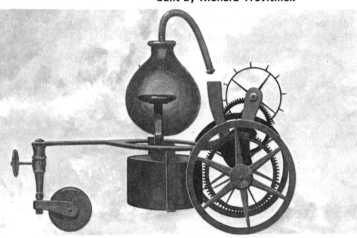

**The locomotive *Catch-Me-Who-Can*
built by Richard Trevithick**

Model of a locomotive, 1775

Trevithick's road locomotive, 1801

How the first steam engines were built

The invention of the steam engine during the eighteenth century had a fundamental effect on man's progress. Some earlier forms of this machine had appeared during the previous century. The most famous were those of Papin whose work provided a great stimulus for research into steam.

Papin built a boat with steam-operated paddles, but builders of sailing boats were hostile to this new craft and Papin could not make much progress with it. However, he had proved what a powerful force steam could be in locomotion. Thomas Newcomen built a steam engine in 1705. It began to be used for pumping water out of mines about six years later, and by 1725 the engine was widely used in collieries. It continued in use for many years although it was not very efficient and worked slowly.

It was James Watt (1736–1819) who examined all the previous efforts and perfected them into a steam engine that worked fast and efficiently. For this engine Watt invented a steam condenser that was separate from the cylinder which worked the piston.

The steam engine had a sensational success and proved itself enormously useful, especially in factories where it replaced machines that had previously been worked by water or animal power. It was eventually used as a locomotive to pull wagons.

How the telegraph wire works

Man has used many ingenious methods to solve the problem of long-range communications. He has used fiery beacons on hilltops (as the ancient Romans did), and smoke signals like the American Indians. But these all became primitive with the invention of the telegraph.

We owe this invention to the work of a number of scientists. As early as 1753 one scientist had written in a Scottish journal about a plan to send messages over a distance by means of electricity. Little attention was paid to the suggestion. It was only during the middle of the nineteenth century that the first telegraph lines came into operation. These were largely the work of the British scientists Wheatstone and Cooke and of the American, Morse.

Basically the telegraph consists of a transmitter which converts a message into electrical signals. The short signals are called dots and the long signals dashes. These dots and dashes travel along the telegraph wires and are picked up by a receiving set. The signals then move a metal point that writes the dots and dashes on a paper tape. These dots and dashes are a code which can later be translated into a written message. From 1850 until the 1920s, when teleprinters came into operation, Morse was the code most used. The telegraph is being superseded by computer networks.

How modern surgery was developed

Modern surgery has a vast range of techniques to treat diseases in man. One of the main factors in its development was the discovery of anaesthetics, the science of making pain disappear.

In 1850 the American dentist Horace Wells discovered the anaesthetic properties of 'laughing gas' and became the founder of a new science. It became possible for lengthy operations to be carried out on patients without their feeling any pain at all.

During the first half of the twentieth century surgery often achieved results that were almost miraculous. Harvey Cushing, an American neurosurgeon, was one of the first men to open the human skull and perform brain surgery on tumours, abscesses and other disorders. Another American, A. Blalock, was one of the first surgeons to operate on the heart. This is a branch of surgery where major developments have occurred, leading to the heart transplants of today. Plastic surgery can now work wonders and rebuild new faces for persons who have been disfigured in serious accidents.

Coal train pulled by the steam engine *Locomotion* on the Stockton-Darlington Line

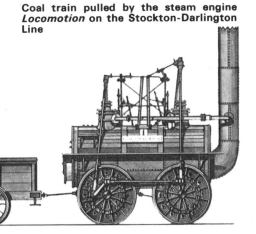

The sealed cabin of the space-ship created by Jules Verne

part can cause disaster. As there are stringent weight limitations, all the parts must be as light as possible.

The space shuttle is the kind of space-ship now in use in the United States. It has wings that are used only on landing. At launch, the space shuttle is attached to two booster rockets and a large fuel tank. The booster rockets fire to carry the shuttle up to a height of about 45 kilometres. Then they separate and fall back to Earth beneath parachutes. Using fuel from the fuel tank, the shuttle fires its own rocket engine to attain Earth orbit. The tank is then discarded. At the end of the mission, the shuttle fires its engine to slow its motion and re-enter the atmosphere.

How space-ships are built

The word 'space-ship' has become very familiar Once these vehicles were the creations of the fertile imagination of the writer Jules Verne. Today space-ships are a reality of high technical development.

There are thousands of components that go into the making of a space-ship and their cost runs into millions of dollars. Every component is rigorously tested for reliability as the failure of a single

How an astronaut's space-suit is made

One of the weirdest features in space travel is the space-suit worn by astronauts, with its huge

The American *Skylab* space station, which was used by three teams of astronauts in 1973 and 1974

The Russian *Soyuz* space-ship

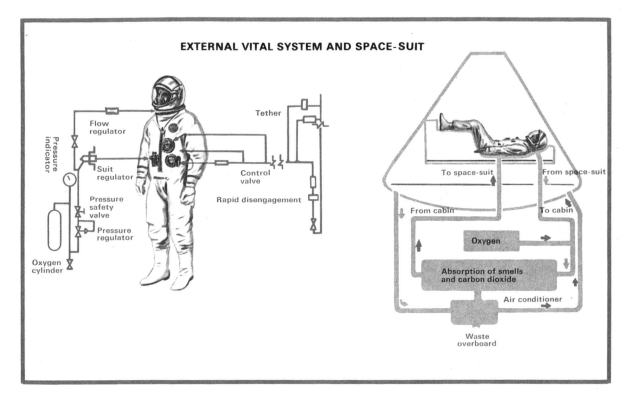

EXTERNAL VITAL SYSTEM AND SPACE-SUIT

spherical helmet, the thick tunic, the bulky gloves and boots and all the various gadgets and fittings.

The space-suit is a highly perfected machine in itself. It consists of no fewer than fifteen layers of special materials to protect the body of the astronaut. The space-

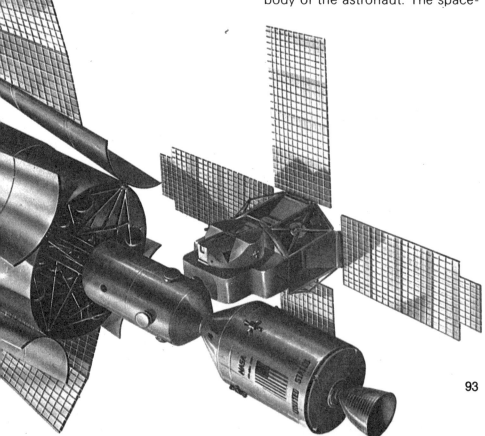

suit must provide oxygen for the astronaut to breathe and protect the astronaut from the vacuum and heat or cold of space. It must also be flexible enough to allow the astronaut to move freely. For travel in space, the astronaut wears an MMU (manned manœuvring unit), which contains small gas-powered thrusters.

The space-suit must also contain food and water supplies, fittings to dispose of bodily wastes and a surface to deflect heat and radiation. The helmet visor requires protective filters to prevent the astronaut from viewing the Sun directly and risking severe dazzling and retinal burns. The suit also has to be fireproofed to the maximum possible extent.

The space-suit took years and millions of dollars to develop.

How methane gas is used

The first experiments in the industrial use of methane gas began about seventy years ago. Further developments took place during the Second World War when natural gas, which is composed largely of methane, was used as a substitute for petrol which was scarce.

The use of methane as a fuel for the internal combustion engine was studied first in France and later in Italy. Today methane is used fairly extensively as a fuel, especially for domestic gas cookers and central heating boilers. The fact that methane can be transported in cylinders, tanks and along pipelines has made it possible to take it to country areas where manufactured gas would be difficult and expensive to obtain.

Methanol and formaldehyde are obtained from methane. Methanol is used as an anti-freeze and formaldehyde as a disinfectant.

There are various ways of locating deposits of methane gas. The most ingenious method is to cause miniature earthquakes through underground explosions. As the explosion occurs scientists measure how long it takes the shock waves to reach the rock layers and travel back again. When these shock waves encounter a zone of liquid and gas deposits, the way they travel changes and special instruments register the change. Once the deposits have been found, the gas is extracted and distributed through pipelines or liquefied and sealed inside metal cylinders.

The geological conditions for oil and natural gas are similar. Exploration for oil in many countries led to the discovery and utilization of vast quantities of gas.

How the tape recorder works

Modern science and technology have made it possible, among other wonderful things, to make a permanent record of sounds and human speech. The tape in a tape recorder is made of an insulation material on which a thin magnetic layer has been placed. The tape is normally 3 millimetres wide in cassettes and 6 millimetres in reels.

How does a tape recorder work?

There is a motor which turns a reel of tape from the supply wheel to the take-up reel. The tape passes across the recording head. When we speak into the microphone the voice is turned into a series of electrical impulses. These impulses are caught on the tape in various patterns. In video tape recordings the light signals are

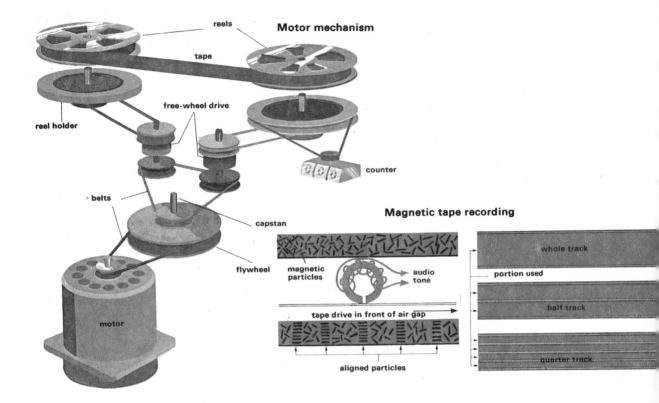

Motor mechanism

reels
tape
free-wheel drive
reel holder
belts
capstan
flywheel
counter
motor

Magnetic tape recording

magnetic particles
audio tone
tape drive in front of air gap
aligned particles
whole track
portion used
half track
quarter track

turned into electrical impulses recorded on the tape.

When the tape is played back it runs past an electromagnet. The magnetic patterns that have been recorded along the magnetized tape set up a variable magnetic field with the electromagnet.

The impulses of this magnetic field are then converted into sounds which are amplified and played through a loudspeaker to re-emerge as the original speech or music that was first fed into the tape recorder.

Today tape recorders are very popular. Besides being easy to operate they have the added advantage that recordings can be erased and the tape used many times.

A new compact type of tape recorder is the cassette recorder. This works on the same principle but uses narrower tape in its own self-contained cassette.

How a film is made

The first step towards making a film is the idea for the subject. The next requirement is money to pay for all the production costs. The producer is the man who raises this money and generally he chooses the director, the most important man in making a film. The director then appoints a writer to prepare a screenplay which is like a stage play but consists of hundreds of short scenes which finally make up the whole film.

A film studio seen for the first time is quite an overwhelming sight. You may see a straight road lined with marble columns representing a Roman road of 2,000 years ago. Near this scene there might be a ramshackle prairie town of the Wild West. In another part of the studio there may be a magnificent governor's palace set in imperial India. The studio is therefore crowded with Roman soldiers or gladiators, cowboys or young English colonial ladies. Some part of the studio will probably be very strictly cordoned off because a film crew may be 'shooting' there.

Today film directors prefer to work on location which means they film their scenes in real places outside instead of creating them from plaster and wood inside a studio. Often film crews with their actors and actresses travel from one continent to another. But when a film is a historical or period piece it is usually shot inside a studio.

Films employ armies of technicians. Skilful carpenters and scene painters build intricate structures known as sets which can be of medieval castles, or of ultramodern apartments.

How the sound track of a film is synchronized with the action

Sometimes films are shot or photographed without sound: the dialogue is added later together with sound effects and other noises. When these sounds are added the noise of a waterfall might be produced by merely shaking water about in a basin or the voice of a stage actor might replace that of the film actor in a process known as dubbing.

The major developments in cinematography were the introduction of sound in 1927 and the advent of colour photography.

The cinema really grew up as an art after the Second World War but it found an extremely dangerous rival in television. So the film industry began to think up counter-attractions. These included the evolution of wide screens as in the processes known as CinemaScope and Cinerama. In wide-screen presentations, a special lens may be used that spreads out the image on the film to fill the screen. When the film is shot, a similar kind of lens is used to squeeze a wide field of view on to standard film. Modern cinemas in addition may also use stereophonic sound which is emitted by numerous loudspeakers. This gives the audience the impression that they are right in the middle of what is happening.

The story of the cinema is not yet finished. Scientists are studying a way of producing satisfactory three-dimensional films so that the images are no longer flat. Experiments have also been carried out with a circular screen that completely surrounds the audience.

How different notes are produced in wind instruments

Wind instruments produce sounds which originate in the breath of the player. These instruments fall into two classes: woodwind and brass. The woodwinds (some of which are actually made of metal, such as silver flutes) comprise the flute, the oboe, the clarinet, the bassoon and others. The brass instruments include the trumpet, the horn, the trombone, and the tuba. The origins of wind instruments are extremely ancient: they began as instruments made from the massive tusks of mammoths. The modern flute consists of a cylindrical tube through which the player blows across a hole. The player opens and closes various other holes in the instrument and

Euphonium

a long metal tube which has been bent into a special shape and fitted with a bell-shaped opening and a cup-shaped mouthpiece.

How a pianoforte works

The pianoforte is a keyboard instrument. The sound is produced by pressing on keys which move little hammers, making them strike against stretched metal strings. For this reason the pianoforte can be grouped as either a percussion or a string instrument.

The pianoforte took several hundred years to perfect. Its ancestors include the spinet, the clavichord, the virginals and the harpsichord. The man generally regarded as having invented the pianoforte was an Italian called Bartolomeo Cristofori (1655–1731). He called his instrument

Bass tuba

Flugelhorn

varies the intensity of his breath in order to obtain the various musical notes.

The oboe, however, is a reed instrument. The air vibrates as it is blown across a double reed fitted to the mouthpiece. The clarinet has a more supple and brilliant sound. The bassoon is the bass member of this musical group. The best known of the brasses is the trumpet. This is really

the *'gravecembalo* that played quietly and loudly' (*piano* and *forte*). The loudness of the sound could be controlled by the pressure of the fingers striking the keys. Pedals were then added to the instrument to control its sound quality. The hammers, which had been previously covered in leather, were later covered in soft felt. These innovations and improvements helped to make the pianoforte much superior in range and quality of sound to other instruments of this group.

How matter is made

Complicated and sensitive instruments enabled modern scientists to approach the problem which had for long absorbed the alchemists of olden days: what constitutes matter.

In the past, scientists believed all matter was made up of tiny particles, each of which was given the name of 'atom' from the Greek meaning 'indivisible'.

Modern scientists have managed to weigh the atom and have also succeeded in examining its structure. They have discovered that the incredibly small world of the atom is like an infinitely small solar system with a sun at the centre and planets revolving round it in different orbits. The sun in this system is called the nucleus and the planets are the electrons.

Today scientists can alter matter by acting on the atomic nucleus: this is what nuclear physics is about. But what exactly is an atom? To understand, we must take any piece of matter: for example, a lump of sugar. We then break up the lump into smaller pieces and those pieces into even smaller pieces. We do this hundreds of thousands of times until we reach particles that are so small that they can no longer be broken down. This basic particle of sugar that we have obtained is called a sugar molecule. Let us imagine that we could grasp one of these molecules and break it up. The molecule would then break up into forty-five pieces consisting of twelve atoms of carbon, twenty-two of hydrogen and eleven of oxygen. The sugar no longer exists: all we have are atoms of carbon, hydrogen and oxygen, the materials of which sugar is made.

If we could break down a molecule of water we would obtain three atoms: two of hydrogen and one of oxygen.

Sugar, water, rocks, metals, wood, food, our bodies and everything in nature, consists of atoms. These atoms are arranged in various groupings to produce different materials and substances.

How an atom is made

Everything is made up of atoms which are the smallest parts of an element still possessing the chemical properties of that element. It is difficult to realize how small atoms are. They have a diameter of about one-hundred-millionth of a centimetre. At one time scientists believed atoms were little spheres that could not be broken, but we know now that atoms are composed of other particles which are even smaller. Each atom is like a miniature solar system: at the centre it has a nucleus which consists of protons and neutrons around which electrons revolve.

The atom consists almost en-

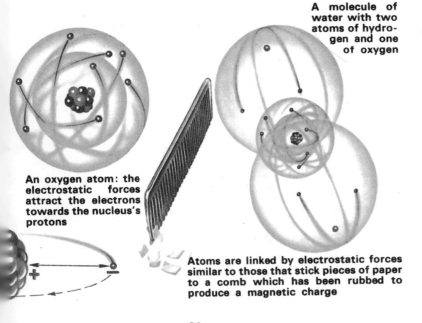

A molecule of water with two atoms of hydrogen and one of oxygen

An oxygen atom: the electrostatic forces attract the electrons towards the nucleus's protons

Atoms are linked by electrostatic forces similar to those that stick pieces of paper to a comb which has been rubbed to produce a magnetic charge

tirely of empty space and its entire size is that of the orbit of its outer electron. This electron, which revolves at extremely high velocity, forms an impenetrable shield. A propeller going round very fast will give us an idea of an electron. The electron seems to be at every point of its orbit at the same time because it goes round the nucleus so fast. That is why we say the atom consists mostly of empty space. The spherical shield formed by the revolving electrons prevents the emptiness between their orbits and the nucleus from being filled in normal circumstances.

The nucleus and the electrons each have a diameter of about one-tenth of a millionth part of a millionth part of one centimetre. Nearly all the mass of the atom is contained within the nucleus. The electrons are very light compared with the protons and the neutrons which are 1,837 times heavier than the electrons.

Electrons have a negative charge and they are fixed to the atom and cannot break away from their orbits through centrifugal force because protons have an equivalent positive charge and the two balance each other. Neutrons have no electrical charge.

How the atom's negative and positive charges are formed

In normal conditions the number of electrons that revolve round the nucleus of an atom is exactly the same as the number of protons. The negative and positive charges are therefore the same and the atom is electrically neutral. But when there is no such balance of positive and negative inside the atom, because an electron has been lost or one extra one has been gained from another atom, the protons in the nucleus can no longer keep the negative-positive balance equal. From that point the atom ceases to be neutral and becomes charged with electricity. The charge is negative if there are too many electrons, and positive if the electrons are fewer in number.

Atoms form various elements according to how many protons and electrons they possess. For example, the atom which has only one proton and one electron forms hydrogen; the atom with two protons and two electrons forms helium; the atom with three of each forms lithium.

In nature, about ninety elements exist, many of them very rare. Other elements have been created artificially by nuclear processes, adding protons and electrons to atoms to form new elements such as einsteinium, mendelevium, nobelium and lawrencium. This last element has 103 electrons and a nucleus of 103 protons.

The nuclear power station at Oyster Creek was the first American one to compete against coal as a source of energy

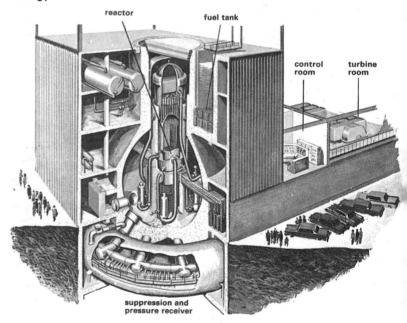

reactor   fuel tank   control room   turbine room

suppression and pressure receiver

How to guard against atomic radiation

Nuclear power was first unleashed in a wave of destruction at Hiroshima and Nagasaki in 1945. As a result of the explosion of the atomic bombs over these Japanese cities, hundreds of thousands of people lost their lives. Many of them were killed by the radioactive waves released by the bombs and even in peacetime people can still be killed by this radiation.

The seriousness of the effect of radiation depends on various factors. These include the size of the radioactive dose received by the body, the duration of the exposure to the radiation, the type of radiation involved and the part of the body affected.

Normally the body can restore and repair any damage done to it but when radiation destroys the cells and tissues they cannot be replaced.

For this reason people who work in scientific laboratories and industries dealing with radioactive materials must be carefully protected with special clothing and equipment and have frequent health checks.

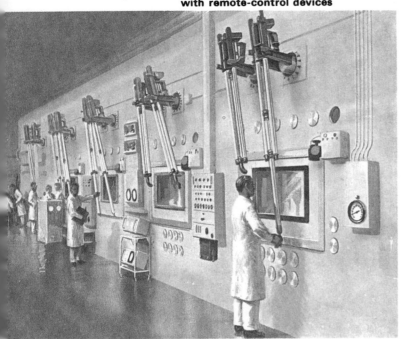

Radioactive materials in research reactors must be handled at a safe distance and with remote-control devices

After taking a shower (above) a technician is checked with a Geiger counter (below)

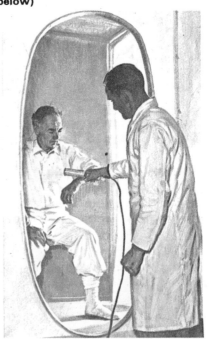

How a nuclear reaction takes place

We speak of a nuclear reaction whenever the nucleus of an atom undergoes any change in its properties. For example, this could be the loss of one or more protons or other particles from within the nucleus, which in turn is possibly caused by the impact of other particles. In nature this process can take place spontaneously in certain substances and gives rise to radioactivity.

Radioactivity was discovered in 1896 by the French scientist Henri Becquerel who proved that pitchblende, a mineral that contains uranium, could darken photographic plates even if they were wrapped in dark paper. It became evident to Becquerel that a very penetrating form of radiation was involved.

We now know that this radiation consists of alpha particles and that radioactive materials also give out two other types of radiation: beta and gamma. Alpha

several centimetres of metal thickness is needed to reduce gamma radiation to an acceptable level.

It was not simple to produce these rays artificially and it took many years of difficult research and complicated experiments. In the end the scientists succeeded. They bombarded the atoms of certain materials with particles taken from naturally radioactive material. By increasing or decreasing this bombardment, the scientists were able to break apart the protective shell of electrons and reach the nucleus of an atom.

In this way nuclear fission, or the splitting of the atom, was achieved. Under such bombardment the atomic nucleus splits into two smaller nuclei. As this happens, some neutrons are ejected by the splitting atomic nucleus and collide with the nuclei of neighbouring atoms. This sets off a chain reaction, releasing enormous quantities of energy which can go out of control with disastrous results.

When a neutron (1) and a uranium nucleus (2) collide (3) the uranium nucleus becomes unstable (4) and divides into

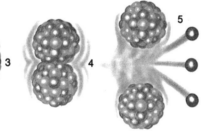

two smaller nuclei which give off neutrons and energy to regain stability (5). This is the process of atomic fission

particles are not very powerful and they can be stopped by a thickness of a few sheets of paper or by a few centimetres of air. Beta rays are more penetrating but can be stopped by thick cardboard, a few metres of air or thin sheet metal. Gamma rays, like X-rays, are extremely penetrating and can be very dangerous to plant and animal life. To stop them

How nuclear reactors are fuelled

Nuclear reactors are complicated structures in which the chain reaction from atomic fission can be set off, continued and kept under control. In this way, an atom can be split without the risk of a terribly destructive explosion. Instead, the process is done gradually and a large amount of energy is produced.

Nuclear reactors are fuelled in different ways. Nuclear fuel must always be a substance which can set off a chain reaction when bombarded with neutrons. The most commonly used elements in fuelling reactors are uranium, plutonium and thorium.

At the heart of the reactor there is the moderator which is a substance that slows down the speed of the neutrons and regulates their flow. The reactor is called fast if it uses fast neutrons and thermal if the neutrons have been slowed down, thereby transferring much of their energy to the moderator.

Fast reactors burn plutonium produced in thermal reactors. They can also generate plutonium from natural uranium or from used uranium

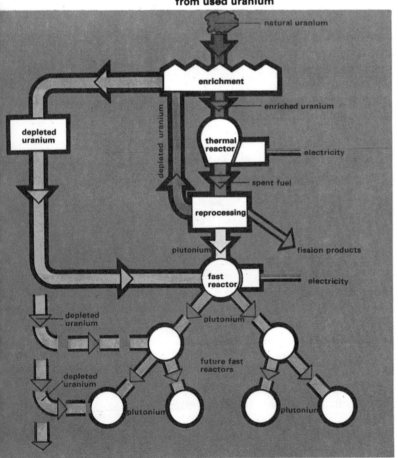

How uranium for nuclear reactors is produced

Uranium in its natural state is found in quantities that average about 4 grammes to every ton of rock. It is an extremely expensive process to extract this mineral from the rocks that contain it even when the deposits are relatively rich.

The best material for nuclear fission is Uranium 235, but natural uranium has only one atom of this structure for every 140 atoms of Uranium 238. So even when the uranium has been extracted from rocks, the element has to be further processed to get the portion with the atomic structure needed for nuclear reactors.

Once the atomic reaction has been set in motion, the energy which is released mostly takes the form of heat. This heat is led to a type of boiler where it generates steam that is later put to several uses. One kilogramme of uranium yields as much energy as 3 million kilogrammes of coal.

How nuclear energy can be used

The splitting of an atom produces a huge amount of energy and scientists from the very beginning have studied ways of harnessing this power to serve mankind. It was from such studies that the first atomic piles or reactors were built.

In 1942 Enrico Fermi and his colleagues became the first to make this major conquest. But a world war was raging and the first use that the energy from nuclear fission was put to was the atomic bomb. Later, however, this new source of energy was placed in the service of man.

Today the heat produced in atomic reactors is used to generate electric power. Soon, whole cities could be heated by nuclear power stations, the waters of the seas could be desalinated and made fresh by atomic power and the world's deserts irrigated so that they become fertile. Nuclear power has already been harnessed to power the engines of ships and submarines.

The various radioactive materials produced in reactors are now employed in many ways to aid mankind. They have helped doctors to treat dangerous diseases and farmers to produce more and better crops. Atomic science can also be used to explore the Earth and help us find its still hidden stores of riches.

Another use of atomic power is to preserve foodstuffs for longer periods and this will help man to deal with the problems of world hunger in the future.

The splitting of the atom has opened up a new era for the world.

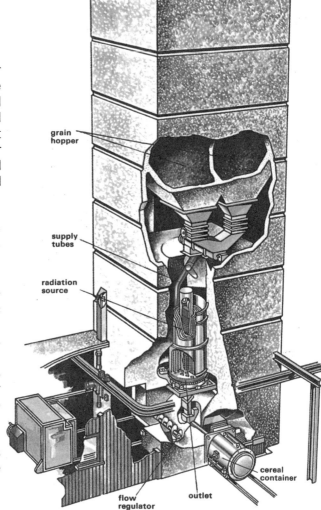

grain hopper

supply tubes

radiation source

flow regulator

outlet

cereal container

Machine for radiating cereals at Iskenderun in Turkey uses Cobalt 60 to prevent insects from breeding in the cereals

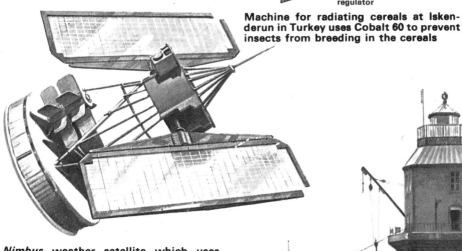

Nimbus **weather satellite which uses solar batteries as a source of power**

The lighthouse at the entrance of Baltimore harbour is powered by 225,000 curies of Strontium 90 and is automated

How computers are used in industry

The electronic computer is used in many fields of activity and is extremely valuable in doing complicated work accurately and quickly. It has removed much of the drudgery from such routine tasks as telephone switchboard operation, the working of lifts, and book-keeping.

How do these wonderful machines work? We can see in the simple example of checking the stocks held by a warehouse.

The diagram on this page shows the various operations that take place one after the other. In large-scale industries it costs a great deal of money to keep a large number of goods in store. Nevertheless a company must always know how many goods it has at a given time in case it runs out of any item. So there must always be a reserve level below which stocks must not go. When that level is reached the company orders more goods to be delivered.

One way of keeping a check is to use a punched-card system. Each article which is delivered to the warehouse has its own card punched with the required information which may relate to style, colour, price, size or other relevant details, and this is fed into the computer.

When the article is sold and leaves the warehouse the computer is fed with this information too. At any time the computer can show exactly how many of those articles are in stock and if the stocks have to be replenished. The computer does this job with great speed and accuracy and can give an account of exactly how many articles of many different types are in stock.

The initial effect of computers is as an efficient means of performing complicated or routine tasks. In the long term, however, they will make new and different activities possible. For instance, education and many occupations will be greatly affected as methods of storing and retrieving vast quantities of information are further developed.

Flow chart for computerized stores

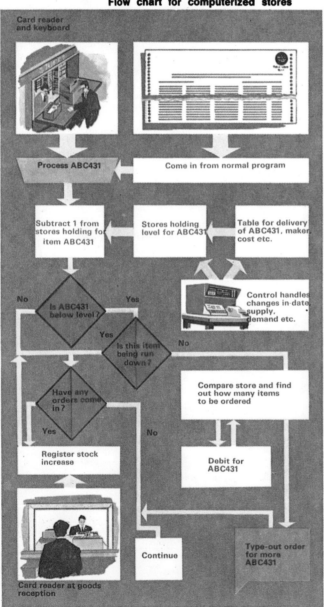

Card reader and keyboard

Process ABC431

Come in from normal program

Subtract 1 from stores holding for item ABC431

Stores holding level for ABC431

Table for delivery of ABC431, maker, cost etc.

Is ABC431 below level? No / Yes

Is this item being run down? Yes / No

Control handles changes in date, supply, demand etc.

Have any orders come in? No / Yes

Compare store and find out how many items to be ordered

Register stock increase

Debit for ABC431

Continue

Type-out order for more ABC431

Card reader at goods reception

How computers work

All computers work in basically the same way. They follow a set of instructions called a program that enables them to do calculations on information fed into them. This process produces a result that is used in some way. The great advantage of computers over other machines is that the program can be changed, so that a computer can be given a wide variety of tasks to perform.

Computers consist of four main units – an input unit, a central processing unit, a memory unit and an output unit. The central processing unit is at the centre of operations and generally consists of a microchip located in the computer case. It controls the operations of all the other units, which may be part of the computer or connected to it.

The input unit is used to feed information or data into the computer. It is usually a keyboard, but it may also be a light pen that interacts with a computer screen, or simpler devices such as a joystick, a mouse or a bar-code reader. The keyboard is also used to write programs.

The central processing unit first passes the information to the internal memory, where it is held temporarily. The program is also held in the memory, and the processing unit follows the program to produce the results. These go to the output unit, which is usually a video screen or printer, or they may be sent along telephone lines to other computers.

The computer also has an external memory unit such as disc drive that takes programs and data from the internal memory and records them for use at a later date.

How the various chemicals got their names

The complicated but accurate system of naming the various chemical substances that we use today was first drawn up 200 years ago by a brilliant French scientist, Antoine Lavoisier, who is generally regarded as the father of modern chemistry.

Lavoisier was the first scientist to recognize the importance of

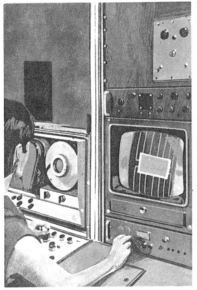

Computerized systems can be used in the design of components

oxygen in the process of combustion or burning. He laid down the principle of the conservation of matter which stated 'nothing is created, nothing is destroyed'.

But the work of Lavoisier did not end there. In collaboration with three other scientists, he devised a reformed system of chemical terminology in 1787, giving a precise name to every known chemical substance. To him we owe a name like 'ferrous oxide' which tells us immediately what substances are involved, in this case iron and oxygen. Before Lavoisier, early scientists had used peculiar and fantastic names to identify the various chemicals.

How timber is transported through forests

Today huge trees can be felled with special tools that work very quickly and the entire operation is carried out by teams of specially trained lumbermen according to well organized plans. Methods of felling trees and converting them into logs are much the same in all forested areas.

One important consideration in lumbering is not to destroy an entire forest, but to cut down only mature trees and leave room for the younger ones to grow. In this way forests, which are part of our priceless heritage, can be kept alive.

Once a tree has been felled, the branches are removed with axes or special saws. The trunk is then cut into sections of the desired length and the bark stripped. The wood should then be left to season in the forest for a period ranging from three months to a year. Seasoning allows wood to dry gradually and thus avoids much of the cracking and splitting which can spoil it.

After the seasoning comes the problem of transporting the timber from the forest. Wood can be carried by lorry, railway trucks or river craft. But large pieces of timber are extremely difficult to transport, particularly if there are no roads and the terrain is rough.

One old method was to cut out 'channels' through a forest which followed steep slopes. The big logs would then be pushed along these channels and slid down the slopes.

This method damaged much of the wood and today timber is carried through forests by means of overhead cables. These are expensive to instal but they move considerable quantities of timber quickly and thus recover their initial cost.

How the electric battery was invented

The first electric battery was born as a result of one of the most famous scientific disputes. During the eighteenth century the Italian doctor Luigi Galvani of Bologna carried out a series of interesting experiments on dead frogs. Galvani obtained vibrations in the muscles of the animals hung from copper hooks over an iron rod. From these twitchings Galvani deduced that the frog possessed electric properties. He was mistaken in thinking this.

But Galvani's work was valuable even though it produced faulty conclusions because it opened the way to the study of electricity by such scientists as Alessandro Volta, another Italian. Volta turned Galvani's theory on its head by saying

A simple battery generates electromotive force as the result of a chemical process

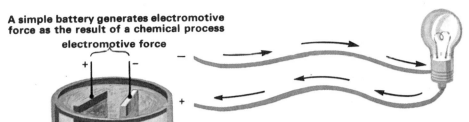

electromotive force

carbon — electrolytic solution — zinc

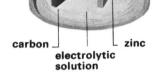

zinc covering — sal-ammoniac paste — carbon cylinder

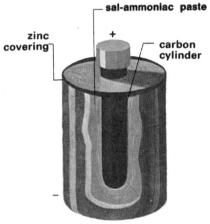

Commercial dry battery

Car battery (accumulator)

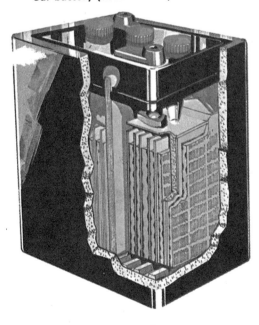

that the frog had 'conducted' electricity which had been generated in the contact between the two metals.

After many fierce arguments Volta won the day. Using his own theories he went on to invent the electric battery by placing zinc and copper in a bath of acid water and so provided a source of continuous current.

Modern physics has revealed the real nature of electricity, a mysterious force which has been known to man since the earliest times. All substances in which the atoms have been placed out of balance because they lack certain electrons or because they have too many electrons, are either positively or negatively charged. Positive charges are composed of atoms or molecules which have lost one or more electrons. Negative charges consist of atoms which for some reason have more than their normal number of electrons.

Electrons which pass from one atom to another inside a material such as a copper wire, form an electric current. This current flows extremely fast from one end of the wire to the other.

When the current flows in the same direction it is known as direct or D.C. This is the type of current generated in a battery. When the electric current changes its flow to a well defined frequency it is known as alternating or A.C. A.C. current is used for lighting and for domestic and industrial purposes.

THE HOW OF ANCIENT PEOPLES

How the hanging gardens of Babylon were built

According to the stories of the time the hanging gardens of Babylon began as a gesture of love and affection. Nebuchadnezzar, king of Babylon from 605 to 562 B.C., had married a Mede princess who was very homesick for her native land and its greenery. To please her the king created the most beautiful gardens on the terraces of his royal palace.

The ancient peoples considered these gardens as one of the seven wonders of the world. Archaeologists have never found any trace of them but some writers who saw the gardens have left behind detailed descriptions. They were not literally 'hanging' but were 'up in the air', that is roof gardens laid out on a series of terraces. These terraces were supported on strong vaults and were filled in with soil in which many kinds of trees grew.

The biggest danger to these gardens was rain which in that region occurs in downpours at certain times of the year. To protect the gardens from the torrential rain the vaults were covered in bitumen or resin and clad in sheets of lead.

During the dry season the gardens were irrigated by pumps from the river Euphrates. The water was brought from ground level to a tank placed on the highest terrace.

How old chemist shops developed

Today a chemist shop is not much different from any other shop. It has shelves which display a wide variety of goods in packets of various colours. Many of the prescriptions which a doctor gives us can be dealt with by an ordinary assistant in the chemist shop.

It was not always like this: at one time a chemist shop was a real workshop or laboratory where medicines were made by mixing together carefully all the various ingredients named in the prescription. These establishments were known as apothecaries. Their shelves were lined with elegant pots of glass or porcelain which contained medicines or poisons. In the rear of the premises the apothecary would pound herbs and grains of medicine together with a pestle and mortar. He measured out the correct doses on a set of scales, made up pomades or pastes and ointments, prepared elixirs or poultices, pills and laxative powders.

Many of the drugs used were of plant origin and are still employed today. But some of the cures were absurd and revolting and used only by gullible patients.

A highly educated woman like Madame de Sévigné, for example, still believed at the end of the seventeenth century that the blood of a female adder purified and toned up the human organism.

The adder's blood, together with dozens of other ingredients, provided a very famous antidote which appears to have first been made up in the days of the Emperor Nero and used until modern times.

How the ancient Germans lived

The peoples who lived between the Rhine and the Danube were considered by the ancient Romans to be barbaric and were called Germans.

The Germans were of mixed Slavic and Teutonic origin. They were divided into numerous tribes, many of which were nomadic while others lived in squalid little villages. Most Germans lived by breeding animals such as sheep and cattle but they also looted and plundered. Their social system was rough and ready. There were three classes: the freemen warriors, the half-free and the serfs or slaves.

Tribal chiefs were elected by the warrior class. This class also declared war, ordered migrations, shared out booty. The Germans had no written laws or judges. Whoever had a wrong done to him had the right to personal revenge and the blood feuds which arose could be passed on from father to son. Disputes could also be settled by payment of an amount considered to be appropriate to the offence involved.

The religion of the ancient Germans was also primitive. They worshipped the forces of Nature. They had great respect for warriors and warlike deeds and force.

Our knowledge of the ancient Germans comes from Julius Caesar's *De Bello Gallico* (The Gallic War). Another extremely valuable source of information is *Germania*, a book published in A.D. 98 by the Roman historian Cornelius Tacitus.

Ancient coins were usually cast by hand around the time of Caesar, and many of these have since been found all over Europe

How the ancient alchemists worked

Alchemists were strange persons: originally metal workers, they became a mixture of scientists, witches and frauds. Simple people were afraid of them and alchemists were often expelled from cities and countries.

Inside their mysterious laboratories alchemists worked with retorts, alembics (the apparatus once used in distilling), burners and jars containing the oddest range of materials. These included precious stones, animals' paws, human bone and stuffed birds.

Alchemists had two aims: to discover the philosopher's stone and the panacea. The first of these was supposed to turn any base metal such as lead into gold. The second was an elixir, or liquid, that would cure every disease. From such dubious persons chemistry eventually evolved.

How the ancient Greeks prayed

The Greeks never formed a single state and every city (known as a *polis*) was independent of the others. But although they were divided politically, the Greeks were aware that they formed one people who shared the same language, even though it had various dialects, and the same religion.

The Greeks were polytheists which means they believed in many gods. These gods and goddesses had human characteristics, including faults, and the Greeks believed that they lived on the top of Mount Olympus, one of the highest mountains in Greece.

To these gods men had to offer sacrifices of animals or the choicest farm produce. Many Greek cities, moreover, celebrated religious feasts which were attended by Greeks everywhere. The most famous of these events were the Olympic Games, held in honour of Zeus, which were celebrated every four years at Olympia.

During this feast there were sacred games in honour of the supreme god. The winning athletes became famous throughout Greece and often poets wrote odes in their praise.

The Greeks also often went to temples which had oracles, a sort of divine presence that gave advice or foretold the future, like the famous one at Delphi.

How the palace of Knossos was built

The royal palace of Knossos in Crete was a true city within a city. The palace was built around an enormous courtyard and contained more than a thousand rooms. It also had a rectangular open-air theatre, perhaps used for ritual performances.

The palace had an ingenious system of plumbing for bringing drinking water and for flushing away waste materials. Light was supplied from above by 'light wells' and colonnaded porticoes provided ventilation. The palace was also the home of all the workers and craftsmen who produced all the tools and equipment needed at court.

The artisans of Crete were excellent ceramicists and potters and their vases were exported to all parts of the Mediterranean. The high level of civilization that developed on Crete had a major influence on neighbouring lands, especially on the Achaeans, the ancestors of the ancient Greeks.

How the ancient Cretans wrote

So far no one has been able to decipher the writing of ancient Crete of which there are many examples. Nearly 2,000 thin, clay tablets were found at the palace at Knossos. It was the first writing in which the characters run from left to right. Sometimes, however, when the writing reached the end of a line it continued in the next line from right to left.

Cretan writing is still silent but the remains so far found are eloquent witness of a flourishing and highly developed civilization.

How the legend of the minotaur was born

The site of the city of Knossos and the imposing ruins of the royal palace with its great number of rooms, passages and tunnels, recall the legend of the minotaur.

The minotaur was a monster, half bull, half man. It lived in the famous labyrinth or maze which was a building composed of an intricate series of corridors and passages. Anyone entering the labyrinth found it impossible to get out again.

Every year the Cretans sacrificed seven maidens and seven youths to the minotaur. These young victims were sent from Athens in Greece which had been conquered by King Minos of Crete.

An Athenian, Prince Theseus, decided the sacrifices must stop and he came face to face with the monster. Theseus killed the minotaur and succeeded in getting out of the labyrinth with the help of Princess Ariadne, daughter of King Minos, who had fallen in love with him.

Greek coin showing the labyrinth

It is difficult to say how this legend began. It is one of the most famous stories in Greek mythology. Perhaps one of the clues lies in the fact that Knossos had an arena in which tauromachy, or bull-fights, took place. In these fights the bull-fighter had to grasp the charging bull by the horns and leap over its back so that it could not gore him.

Painting showing Theseus slaying the minotaur

How the first roads were built and what they looked like

When man began to till the soil and do other kinds of work he left the cave that had been his home and built a house. These houses soon gathered together to form villages which dotted the countryside, and then the problem arose: how were the villages to keep in touch with each other? By this time man had learned to trade goods for other articles he needed and these goods had to be carried to the places where the exchange was done. Man found that he had to prepare special tracks to travel along. The tracks had to be smooth so that the goods would not be damaged by too much bumping and jogging.

With the invention of the wheel man began to travel much faster. The roads had to be improved for wheels could become bogged down in mud or loose soil.

At this point man realized that earth which had been pressed down flat was not enough and a paved road was necessary. The ancient Greeks were already building such roads. These roads had long sunken tracks in them which acted rather like a railway track to take the wheels of vehicles such as carts and chariots. But the true inventors and builders of the modern road were the ancient Romans.

The Romans solved the basic problems of road engineering by using techniques which still hold good today. They learned much from the Etruscans, but they introduced many modifications and improvements.

The Romans cambered or curved the surface of their roads to allow rain water to drain away.

They built a solid foundation by constructing an agger, or embankment, of packed earth or rocks. The top surface of the road rested on the agger and consisted of flat paving stones or gravel. Roman roads were usually about 5 metres wide but some were up to 10 metres. The roads were straight and were used to connect all the main centres of the Roman Empire.

How beer was first brewed

Beer is an alcoholic drink which has been made since ancient times. Man probably learned how to make beer much earlier than he discovered that the juice of the grape could be made into wine.

Beer-making was once a simple household task and families brewed their own supply. Today brewing is a major industry catering for millions of people throughout the world. The industry uses the most up-to-date and complex equipment and must follow strict rules of hygiene. But the basis of brewing remains the same as it did 5,000 years ago: beer is obtained by fermenting the mash obtained by mixing water with barley which has malted or sprouted after being kept in a dark, warm, moist atmosphere. It is from this thick cloudy mash that the clear, sparkling and refreshing drink finally comes.

How the adulteration of food was opposed in the past

The faking or doctoring of foodstuffs is not a modern thing: it has gone on for centuries.

One of the most commonly doctored of foods was bread. Unscrupulous bakers would mix real wheat flour with other worthless powder and this would make bread seem to be of the right weight but such loaves were harmful to health.

To avoid the risk of such doctored food people began to avoid bakers and made their own bread at home. The commercial baker's task was limited to baking the dough which had already been prepared at home.

The miller was another tradesman who was suspected of cheating by mixing powders with flour. The distrust of such food merchants continued until the seventeenth century.

Today in many countries there are regulations ensuring that bread is made to the required standards of weight, quality and hygiene.

How cast iron was first made

Cast iron is an alloy of iron and carbon. The Chinese are generally thought to have produced the first objects of this metal in 513 B.C., while the first iron foundry in England has been recorded in Lincolnshire in A.D. 1161.

It was during the fourteenth century that the importance of cast iron became evident in metallurgy. Cast iron was first used to make cannon balls and then to make the cannons themselves and thirty of these weapons were made at the Siegen foundry in Germany.

As technology improved it became possible to make cast iron tubes. During the sixteenth century the first cast iron stoves appeared as well as tubes and pipes for carrying water.

It was not until the eighteenth century, however, that cast iron achieved a position of real importance. Larger furnaces had to be built to make it and water power was used to work the bellows system to produce the great heat needed in the furnaces. Soon many foundries employing hundreds of workers began to produce cast iron.

Mining in the sixteenth century

How the writings of the ancient peoples came down to us

No ancient Greek or Roman book has ever come down to us. Many were lost among the papyruses and the parchments that perished

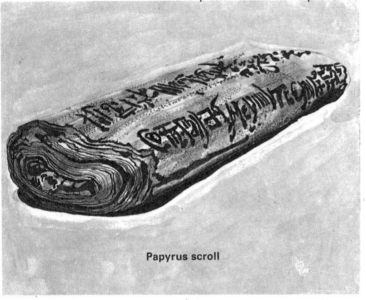

Papyrus scroll

in the fires and destruction in which the once mighty Roman Empire fell. Others were destroyed

Scribe seated with a papyrus open across his lap, from Giza, Egypt, about 2000 B.C.

by the slower but still sure action of time. But before these books vanished from the world many were copied by ancient scribes and scholars.

Much of this work was done by monks during the Middle Ages, especially the Benedictines. During the fourth century St. Jerome had exhorted monks to perfect their art of writing. In the centuries that followed every monastery had its *scriptorium* or writing room. This room was usually next to the library and only the senior monks, the librarian and copyist monks were allowed into it.

Absolute silence reigned in the room as the monks copied out the manuscripts carefully. The silence was broken only when one monk would dictate the contents of a manuscript for the other monks to write down.

How shorthand was born

Ever since man first began to use the letters of the alphabet he has tried to make writing as rapid an act as possible, to keep up with human speech at its normal speed.

The first stenographer, or shorthand writer, was Tiro, the Greek secretary of the famous ancient Roman orator, Cicero. Modern shorthand, however, began in England when Dr. Timothy Bright published his book on the subject in 1588. Many systems using symbols instead of letters and words were later invented.

People normally say 180 words a minute when they speak. Most shorthand writers can write down 120 words a minute, and the highest speeds are about 350 words but these can only be kept up for short periods. Pitman and Gregg, named after their inventors, are two of the best-known shorthand systems. There are also machines that write shorthand: they resemble adding machines and are operated by keys.

How the ancient Romans wrote

The Latin alphabet was largely similar to the one we use today. That alphabet evolved during several stages from the ancient Greek alphabet and spread throughout the Roman world to become the official script of the Empire. The Roman alphabet became even more widespread with the rise of Christianity and the Church helped to extend its use.

In the 2,000 years it has been in existence, the alphabet has undergone several changes to meet varying needs of pronunciation and expression.

How monasteries first appeared

During that period of history known as the Dark Ages after the fall of the Roman Empire, it seemed as if all forms of charity and justice had died. Endless wars raged, killing thousands of people and the arts and learning seemed as if they would vanish.

It was at this time that the first monasteries appeared. They soon spread throughout Europe and became islands of peace which were respected even by barbarian hordes. Monasteries often provided shelter from danger; they helped during famines; they acted as centres of culture and religious faith and as schools for many young people.

Many gifted people who had tired of the rough life in the world at large lived in monasteries. Some of these people were rich and donated their lands to the monks.

The ruins of many famous monastries remain. Among the best known are Fountains Abbey in Yorkshire, founded by the Cistercians in 1132, and the Cathedral Priory at Durham, which the Benedictines founded in 1093.

How blue dye was once made

Marco Polo, the Venetian traveller, merchant and explorer, wrote of the method he saw used in the East to extract the dye from the indigo plant which grows wild in India and other parts of Asia.

Indigo contains a beautiful blue colour which was used in dying clothes long before Marco Polo saw it. In America, for example, garments dyed with indigo have been found in the ancient tombs of the Incas of Peru. The ancient Egyptians also knew about the indigo plant and garments dyed with it have been found in tombs dating back 4,000 years. According to Julius Caesar the ancient Britons used indigo which they obtained from the woad plant.

There are about 300 different varieties of the indigo plant, some growing only in America while others are found only in Asia. The oldest method of extracting indigo from the plant is to grind the plant up in vessels containing water and ammonia. A yellowish liquid is produced, which changes colour as oxygen from the air enters it. It then deposits a muddy sediment at the bottom of the vat which is the actual dye used to colour cloth.

Until the end of the nineteenth century indigo dye was obtained entirely from plants, but today it is mostly produced by the chemical industry.

How the theatre began

The historians of ancient Greece have left descriptions of feasts in honour of Dionysus, the god of wine and merriment. During these feasts a kid, or baby goat, was slain as a sacrifice to the god and the so-called 'goat-song' was performed. One of the priests would sing the tale of Dionysus and the other priests would respond in a chorus. It was from these religious performances that the classical drama and the theatre were born. The ancient Greek

Reconstruction of a Roman theatre at Ostia

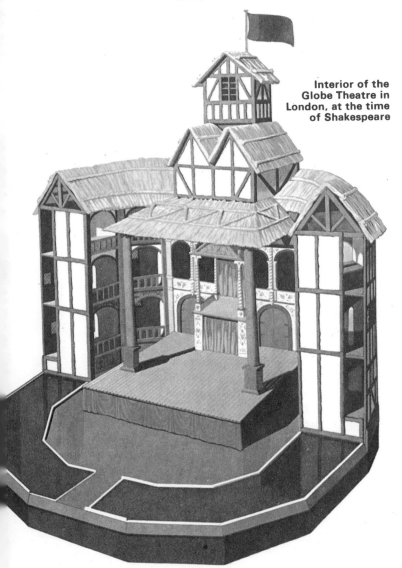

Interior of the Globe Theatre in London, at the time of Shakespeare

word for 'goat-song' is *tragodia* from which our word 'tragedy' comes.

Tragedy was the first form of drama. It took its themes from religion and the many myths and legends about the gods and great heroes like Ulysses and Achilles. The stories were declaimed by the chorus leader and the chorus responded. Gradually two men played the part of the leader and in this way dramatic dialogue was born.

The Greek theatre was in the open air. The actors wore masks, motley tunics and short cloaks. The masks, which they held in front of their faces as they recited their lines, bore grotesque expressions and also helped the actor to project his voice. The ancient Greeks produced great tragic dramatists like Sophocles, Aeschylus and Euripides who exalted the virtues of the gods and heroes.

Comedy, which was developed later, dealt with human foibles and weaknesses such as greed, gluttony, pride and the lust for power. Comedy was also invented by the Greeks and one of the greatest authors in this field was Aristophanes.

Right: eighteenth-century façade of the Drury Lane Theatre in London
Below: plan of the Palladian Theatre at Vicenza

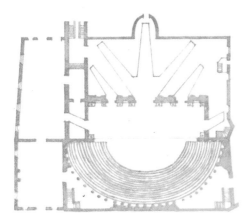

How the word 'laconic' originated

The word 'laconic' today refers to a person who uses few words to express himself. The meaning of this word goes back to the days of Sparta.

Sparta was one of the most important of the city-states in Laconia in the Peloponnese. This region had been occupied by the Dorians who had turned the local inhabitants into a subject people. The lawgiver Lycurgus gave Sparta an aristocratic constitution by which all the people were divided into three classes: the Spartiates (members of the ruling class), the perioeci (the original inhabitants of Laconia, who were considered free, and given civil rights but not political ones) and the helots (slaves). The Spartiates devoted their lives to war and were trained to use weapons from infancy.

When children were seven years old they were taken from their mothers and given to the state so that they could be trained in gymnastics to make their bodies strong. The Spartans were able to stand up to hunger, thirst, cold, heat and fatigue. They were taught to respect the old and to express themselves in as few words as possible, namely, in a laconic manner.

At the age of twenty the young men began their real military service and it lasted practically all their lives. The Spartan way of life was one which banished all forms of luxury and ease. Their way of life was, therefore, in a certain sense, also laconic.

Municipal Theatre, Malmö

117

How writing and hieroglyphics were first used

The first type of writing was a series of pictures. In this figurative script, primitive man made a note of the objects in his life and recorded them on rocks. This type of writing could be read by anyone because it did not represent words but images.

But this system of writing could only represent the simplest concrete ideas such as 'animal', 'water', 'food' and 'drink'. Once man became more civilized he had to find a better type of writing to express such intangible ideas as 'happy', 'balance' or 'freedom'.

It took thousands of years before man evolved a system of words and letters to express his ideas. Pictures developed in two ways: as pictorial art, reproducing the objects and events of the surrounding world; and as writing in which signs eventually became symbols for language. Figurative writing became ideographic or hieroglyphic with the ancient Egyptians.

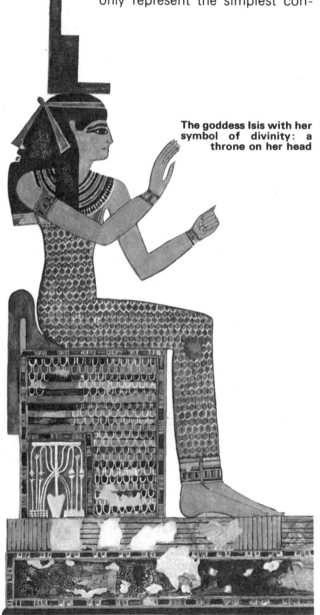

The goddess Isis with her symbol of divinity: a throne on her head

How the first alphabet was born

In man's first attempts to write every mark represented a word: to write 'bird' the writer drew a bird and for 'man' the figure of a man was drawn. Actions also had to be represented in writing: to describe the action of fighting in writing the figure of a man wielding a club was drawn; to express the idea of freshness, a jar of sparkling water was drawn. The ancient Egyptians made further progress in writing but they never created a true alphabet.

Nobody really knows who drew up the first alphabet. It could have been the Semites who first saw Egyptian hieroglyphics in about 1500 B.C. The Semites probably borrowed some of these signs to represent certain sounds made in their own language. These signs were later modified by the Phoenicians and spread throughout the ancient world. The alphabet was an invention which proved to have enormous practical value. With only about twenty simple signs man could write any sort of message. With hieroglyphics and cuneiform (the wedge-shaped writing used by the Babylonians and Assyrians), which still used images and symbols, hundreds of signs were needed.

The function of the alphabet is to convert into signs the various sounds we utter in speech. These sounds are few. Before any alphabet came into existence written signs tried to express whole words, which were many.

The alphabet passed from the Phoenicians to the Greeks who added various letters. The Etruscans then took it over, then the Romans until it came down to us. The word 'alphabet' itself comes from the first two letters of the Greek alphabet: 'alpha' and 'beta'.

Stele, or inscribed slab, in the Louvre Museum in Paris telling the story of Princess Bakhtan and dating from about 200 B.C.

How the Romans regarded the barbarians

The term 'barbarian' meant in ancient Greece and Rome anyone who did not belong to these two great civilizations. The word did not acquire a disparaging meaning until much later. When Rome's empire began, about 800 years after the foundation of the city, to reach its peak of greatness, barbarian people were those who could not describe themselves as Roman citizens.

Rome had many contacts with barbarian people during its thousand years of history, for territorial expansion enabled the Romans to come in contact with them. Particularly important in their relation to the Roman Empire were the Germans who lived in central Europe and were divided into about forty tribes. Most of our knowledge of the Germans comes from the writings of the Roman historian Tacitus who lived in the first and second centuries after Christ. Tacitus described these people as follows: 'Stern, blue eyes, muscular bodies . . . they are not used to bearing thirst or heat, but because of the climate of their land, they can stand up to cold and hunger.'

Concerning the Germans' social organization, Tacitus said: ' . . . they choose their kings according to their nobility and their captains according to their bravery . . . No one is allowed to condemn anyone to death or to imprison anyone or even to strike anyone except their priests.'

What kept the Germans together? Tacitus wrote: 'The strongest inducement to their bravery lies in their family ties. . . .'

The Germans were proud and warlike. Tacitus wrote: ' . . . they believe, in fact, that it is mere laziness and incompetence to obtain something with sweat when it can be got through bloodshed.'

How the tombs of the pharaohs became known as pyramids

Much of our knowledge about the ancient Egyptians and their way of life comes to us from the ancient Greeks who travelled up the valley of the river Nile. The word 'pyramid' itself comes from Greek. The early Greek travellers saw that these royal tombs resembled in shape the cakes made of flour and honey which they presented to the winners of races in athletic events. These cakes were called *pyramis*.

How the Colossus of Rhodes was made

In about the year 312 B.C., King Ptolemy of Egypt was waging war against King Antigonus of Macedonia. The people of the island of Rhodes were fighting on the side of Ptolemy and were a loyal and brave ally on the sea. Antigonus decided to punish them. In 307 he dispatched against them his son

Demetrius at the head of a huge fleet which transported a large army.

The people of Rhodes defended themselves heroically for twelve months, but without any help from outside the island was doomed to fall. Ptolemy arrived in 300 to the rescue and forced Demetrius to withdraw. To commemorate the event the people of Rhodes built a huge statue near the entrance to their harbour and it became one of the seven wonders of the ancient world. The statue represented the god Apollo and was made of the metal from the weapons left behind by Demetrius.

The statue was built by the sculptor Chares of Lindus who worked on it for twelve years from 292 B.C. The statue was over 30 metres high. Its huge bronze legs were strengthened by masonry in the inside and people could climb to the top of the statue up a winding staircase inside.

At night the statue was lit and acted as a lighthouse for shipping. In 225 B.C. the Colossus was broken off at the knees in a severe quake and it was never rebuilt. When the Arabs attacked Rhodes in A.D. 653, they had the fallen Colossus broken up and the bronze sold for scrap. It was said that it took 900 camels to remove the debris.

How the ships of the adventurous Vikings looked

Excavations have made it possible for us to know how the Vikings built their ships. The fighting ships or longships were shallow, narrow in the beam and pointed at both ends. They had a single large, square sail, although they used

The pyramids of Giza

oars as well, a high prow and a projecting stern. The figurehead of the ship of about A.D. 800, unearthed at Oseberg, was a coiled snake with its head upreared. Another Viking ship, found at Gokstad, dates from about A.D. 900.

Longships had about ten oars a side and seem to have carried twice as many men for fighting as for rowing, that would be a total of some sixty men.

The most famous of the longships was the 'big dragon' of King Canute, built in A.D. 1004. It looked like a huge sea serpent, with a dragon's head at the prow and a high-coiled tail at the stern.

The Viking *hafskip* had fewer rowers than the longship and was sometimes more than 21 metres long and 6 metres wide. On voyages of colonization it would carry wives, children, livestock, stores and as many as thirty men.

The naval power of the Vikings was greatly helped by their levy system which allowed them to call up men to form one of the greatest war fleets of their day.

How the ancient Egyptians practised their religion

The religion of the ancient Egyptians was inspired by nature and by the fertility caused by the flooding of the river Nile. The Sun, the wind and animals that helped man in his labours on the land were also objects of worship.

The chief god was Ra who represented the Sun. Ra was the protector of the pharaoh who was known as 'the son of Ra'. Another important divinity was Osiris. This god was killed, according to a legend, by his brother Set who was jealous of his popu-

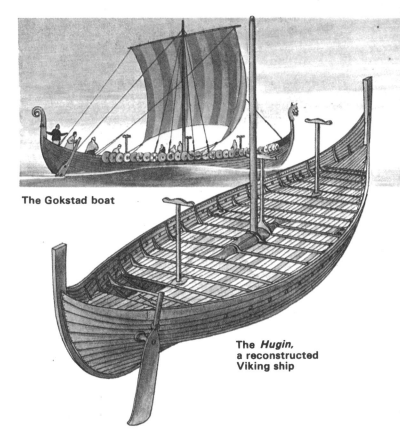

The Gokstad boat

The *Hugin*, a reconstructed Viking ship

The Oseberg ship, an example of a Viking longship

scribes, had the head of an ibis or a baboon.

The Egyptians believed in an after-life in which man was rewarded or punished by Osiris. They thought the soul, Ka, could live on in the after-life if the body was embalmed.

larity among the people. Horus, son of Osiris and of the goddess Isis, avenged the death of his father who rose again and became the ruler of the dead.

The ancient Egyptians worshipped many gods who had the heads or even the whole body of animals: Anubis, the god of graveyards, had the head of a jackal; Apis was a bull which bore the Sun between its horns; Apopis was the wicked serpent, an enemy of Ra and a symbol of the clouds that tried to hide the face of the Sun. Bast was the mistress of love, of matters feminine and of fashion and had the head of a cat; Haket, the divinity that watched over births, had the head of a frog; Kheferi, the scarab god of springs, was represented as a beetle; Khenum, who had a ram's head, was the patron of potters because he was supposed to have fashioned the first man from clay; Mut the goddess was represented by a vulture; Sebek was the crocodile god; Selket was the scorpion goddess; and Thot, the god of

The cat-goddess
Bast or Pasht

How the dead were embalmed in ancient Egypt

The word 'mummy' comes from an ancient Egyptian word meaning 'tar' or 'bitumen'. Egyptian embalmers used many products in their craft such as bees-wax, cassia (a type of cinnamon), juniper oil, onions, palm wine, resin, salt, sawdust, pitch, soda and bitumen to keep the corpses of the rich and the mighty from rotting.

The bodies were wrapped in linen bandages, clothed in funerary garments and adorned with necklaces and amulets. On the face of the deceased there was placed a mask made of rough canvas and chalk, but for dead pharaohs and high dignitaries this mask was made of gold. Poor people were mummified in any haphazard way and paupers were simply thrown without ceremony into a common grave.

The embalmed body of the deceased was buried together with objects which that person had used during his earthly life and which he might need in the next. Naturally, the graves of the dead reflected their social status during life. The tombs of the pharaohs were magnificent structures full of precious treasures and costly objects.

How bell-towers were first made

Bell-towers were first built to contain a bell to summon people to worship in the church or to ring the curfew or a danger signal. They were constructed in such a way that the sound of the bell ringing could be heard as far away as possible.

In the past, church bells used to mark all the main stages of the day such as dawn, dusk and the passage of the hours. Farmers working in the fields would regulate their lives to the sound of the church bells.

Bell-towers are usually tall structures. They can be round, square or many-sided. Gothic bell-towers, also known as steeples, have a long, sharply tapering top called a spire. The great spire of Salisbury Cathedral, built in 1250, is about 125 metres high.

In Italy, most bell-towers are square and are known as campaniles. The earliest are dated between the seventh and tenth centuries and are plain, round towers with a few small, round-arched openings grouped near the top. Round campaniles occasionally occurred in later periods, as in the famous leaning tower of Pisa (begun in 1174) which is a more elaborate version of this type.

How knighthood was obtained

Knighthood began as a military rank. After A.D. 1000 it became a more complicated institution and one of the glorious features of the Middle Ages, the standards of which were both military and religious. One became a knight through birth into the nobility or through bravery in battle. Knights had the right to fight on horseback and this right was bestowed on them in a ceremony by the king. In this ceremony the recipient of the honour would kneel before his sovereign who would touch him on the shoulder with a sword.

The younger children of a feudal lord became knights but first they had to serve a period of service when they were known as squires. The training for knighthood began at twelve years of age. The young squire was taught to ride, to fence and to handle the bow; he also learned to hunt with falcons and dogs. In his teens, the squire had to act as an assistant to a knight, and this was his true apprenticeship. His duties included serving his master at table, looking after his master's horse and weapons, carrying his shield and helping him in battle.

At the age of about twenty the squire became a knight. He spent the whole night before the ceremony awake and in prayer, guarding his arms. This was known as the vigil.

Today knighthood is bestowed on persons by the monarch for outstanding contributions in all spheres of life such as industry, science and the arts. The ceremony of touching the shoulder with the sword is still the same. Knights have the title 'Sir' before their Christian names.

How jousting was held in the Middle Ages

When knights were not away at the wars or carrying out some duty for their lord or king, they displayed their skill and bravery in jousting. This was a sort of tournament held in an enclosed field and was extremely popular in the twelfth and thirteenth centuries when such combats were held on feast days or to celebrate marriages, alliances or victories.

The lord who held the tournament sent his messengers to all the castles in the region, notifying

Jousting in the Middle Ages

them of the event and inviting other knights to take part.

The day of the joust began with the celebration of Holy Mass. The knights challenged one another to fight and the combats took place before a large crowd of excited spectators consisting of the judges, fine ladies and gentlemen and rough countryfolk.

How the knights of old dressed

In the thirteenth century both men and women carried purses or handbags, and gloves, which the ancient Egyptians, Greeks and Romans had all used, were very popular. Ladies often dressed in blue, pink or yellow while the men favoured brown, dark green or turquoise.

The breastplate continued to be the dress of soldiers who also wore a shirt of mail. This shirt was made of small, interlinked, metal rings forming a close network. The soldier's gloves, leggings and shoes were also of mail. The shirt of mail was quite long and was open at the front and the back to allow the soldier to ride on horseback. The knight's armour included the helmet which could be opened or closed. It was closed in battle but there were eye-slits in it to allow the knight to see. The knight's horse also wore a suit of armour.

During the fourteenth century the textile industry in Europe developed considerably. All sorts of beautiful materials such as brocades, silks and velvets appeared on the market. The chemise, a type of smock worn by ladies, also made its first appearance. Women's dresses became longer and longer and ladies employed young men as pages to carry the long trains of their dresses. These dresses had sleeves which clung to the arm but flared out widely at the wrists. During this time the first women's hats and caps appeared.

Order of the Garter

INSIGNIA OF KNIGHTHOOD

Order of the Elephant

Order of the Golden Fleece

125

How dress fashions were in the Middle Ages

The Middle Ages were a period of European history which occurred approximately between the fall of the western Roman Empire in A.D. 476 and the discovery of America in 1492.

During the first three centuries of the Middle Ages, the way people dressed underwent many changes. In the early stages they dressed in the Byzantine fashion: the emperor and the empress wore long tunics in brocade covered with a pallium, a sort of heavy square mantle that had a religious significance. Men let their beards grow and women never cut their hair.

During the Middle Ages, punishment for forgery was savage. Here, a forger is about to have his hand chopped off

When knights prepared for battle they put on a thick, woollen tunic over which they donned their coat of armour or chain mail. They had a broad belt or buckler round their waist from which hung a broad sword. The bandolier went on the right shoulder. On the head was worn an iron helmet, usually with a nose guard, and at the end of the twelfth century the great cylindrical helmet was introduced.

The soldier's dress was completed with a large convex shield on which the knight had his coat-of-arms painted or carved. These arms also decorated the linen surcoat which after about 1200 was worn over the mail shirt.

How women dressed in the sixteenth century

The centre of Europe's fashion for women in the sixteenth century was Italy. It was at this time that gloves became a standard item of dress for women and rich, ornate gloves developed, influenced by the taste of Queen Elizabeth of England. They began to be made in silk or soft leather and decorated with embroidery.

Jewellery was made by such great artists as Benvenuto Cellini. Women wore strings of pearls and ivory combs in their hair. Ladies in other countries impatiently awaited the latest news of the Italian fashions. There were no fashion magazines in those days and models of dresses were shown on dolls.

One of the great fashion designers of this period was Isabella d'Este, Marquise of Mantua. She built her models with the help of famous painters, and the great Leonardo da Vinci is supposed to have given her some ideas. All this luxury was for the nobility and the wealthy, but even the ordinary people dressed smartly enough and the women made themselves up and had their hair styled.

How people dressed during the Renaissance

Dressed in damask and silks, the men of the Renaissance preferred bright colours and often wore costumes of several hues. Towards the end of the fifteenth century, the coat or jacket became shorter and the hose or leggings were elongated. During the sixteenth century men wore a short belted jerkin over a type of skirt.

The novelty for women was the two-piece dress, consisting of bodice and skirt. The skirts were long and wide, edged with ribbon, embroidery or fur.

Wealth was displayed by exaggeration in clothes. Sleeves, sometimes detachable became wider and were often puffed and slashed. The ruff became the most striking feature of both men and women's costume in the second half of the sixteenth century. It was a frill of folded linen worn round the neck and as time passed the ruff grew larger and larger.

During the 1500s women began to wear farthingales. These were underskirts or petticoats made of a stiff material fitted with a hoop round the bottom. They were worn underneath the outer skirt and gave it a wide bell-shape.

How people travelled in coaches

The coach became a widely used form of transport during the eighteenth century when travel was a craze for those who could afford it. They wanted to see new countries and people and were prepared to cover long distances.

Kings, noblemen and the rich had their own personal coaches which were always elegant and comfortable. Their suspension was based on leather straps and later steel springs were introduced which were stronger and more comfortable. Another improvement was the introduction of

This Italian Renaissance interior has a fine chimneypiece with heraldic decoration. Some of the furniture has characteristics of earlier styles, such as Gothic

127

Coach pulled by Cleveland bay horses

windows so that the travellers could see and be seen.

These old coaches seemed to have room for everything. Apart from the passengers there was the baggage, their food, crockery and even a library of books to read on the journey. During the eighteenth and nineteenth centuries a large variety of coaches were built, some had two wheels, others had four. One of the best known was the landau. This was a large, open carriage with four wheels and special seats for footmen and it had hoods which opened in the middle of the body and folded back to either end. The landau was used mainly to travel through the city or on short journeys. It was named after the German city of Landau where it was first made.

People who could not afford the luxury of a carriage of their own travelled with the postal services on coaches called diligences. These were public vehicles that could carry several passengers and ran on regular routes.

How the mysterious Etruscans lived

The Etruscans are the most interesting and the most mysterious of the peoples who lived in Italy before Rome became a mighty empire. They may have come to Italy in about 1000 B.C. from some far region and settled in what is now Tuscany. From there their influence went out to neighbouring regions.

The Etruscan men usually had short beards that came to a point. They wore short, tight-fitting jackets and over these a *tebennus*, a type of cloak that was always brightly coloured and was the precursor of the Roman toga. They had pointed shoes and their caps, known as *tutuli*, were also pointed.

Etruscan women, who were elegant and refined, also wore pointed shoes and caps and long narrow skirts under a pleated mantle. They loved to wear sparkling jewels, earrings, pins, bracelets and pendants of various kinds, often of great beauty and exquisite workmanship, and to comb their hair into various styles.

Etruscan women did not live apart like the women of ancient Greece or, to a lesser extent, of Rome. They took part in gymnastic events and attended banquets.

The guests at an Etruscan banquet were often entertained by musicians playing on flutes and lyres.

The way of life of these people appears to have been happy and carefree. We can tell this from the wall paintings and friezes they left on their tombs and from their sculpture. But we know nothing about the life of the simple Etruscan people who must have worked hard.

How the Etruscans practised their religion

The Etruscans were a very religious people. Their chief gods were Tinia, Uni, Minrva, the trio worshipped by the ancient Romans later under the names of

Two warriors: from an Etruscan wall painting

Apollo of Veii

Jove, Juno and Minerva. Only some of the Etruscan gods had the power to launch thunderbolts. Tinia was one of the more powerful of the divinities.

Religious ceremonies were conducted by priests who formed a very powerful class in Etruscan society. These priests were the only persons permitted to divine or guess the will of the gods and to tell the future. They did this in various ways: by examining the entrails of sacrificed animals; by bird watching; by observing lightning and other weather phenomena; and the ebbing and flowing of streams.

Of all the entrails the liver was studied with the greatest care. A bronze model of a liver found at the city of Piacenza is divided into forty-five areas, each with the name of a presiding deity written in it. The priests who studied birds traced the will of the gods from the way birds flew, cried and ate. The signs seen by these priests were known as auguries which could be either good or bad.

The Etruscan religion comprised a complicated set of beliefs and ceremonies for every act in public life. The laws relating to the foundation of a city were particularly strict.

The Etruscans believed, especially in their early days, that when they died they passed on to another life similar to the one in this world. They provided the dead with many objects of everyday life and the statues on their tombs depict people sitting at table with guests or playing music, singing or even hunting.

How the Etruscans wrote

The origins of the Etruscan language are wrapped in mystery. The Etruscans have left thousands of examples of their writings but most of them are brief inscriptions on their tombs. There have been a few other texts found which were longer and were probably prayers. One of these was discovered on the wrappings of a mummy found in Egypt.

These writings do not tell us very much. The alphabet is similar to the Greek one but the meaning of most of the words is hidden. The main difficulty is that Etruscan does not resemble any other language known to us.

A few words are known: *ati* meant 'mother', *clan* meant 'son', *lautn* meant 'family', *thura* meant 'brother', *sech* meant 'daughter' and *nefts* meant 'nephew'. Other meanings, though not known for certain, were *avil* (year), *mestrev* (magistrate), *spur* (city), *tinsi* (days), *tiv* (moon) and *usil* (sun).

How King Hammurabi became famous

King Hammurabi, ruler of Babylonia, is remembered in many documents as a great lawmaker and warrior. He reigned for some forty years, from about 1792 to 1750 B.C., and made his capital into a city of great splendour.

By using both force and diplomacy Hammurabi extended his rule gradually over all Mesopotamia. His code of laws was a great achievement and gives us an insight into how justice was administered in Assyria and Babylonia.

Hammurabi was also a great soldier and a ruthless leader with a fiery temperament. He loved war but as soon as he had unified his realm he devoted himself to peaceful pursuits and brought great wealth to the nation. His court was frequented by artists, scholars and philosophers. Babylonia became a land of beautiful palaces and buildings such as the temple to the god Marduk which Hammurabi had constructed.

Bas-relief dating from 600 B.C. showing an Assyrian king on horseback

How justice was administered in Babylonia

We know exactly all the 282 laws in which King Hammurabi included the entire legal traditions of his day because they were found on a stele (stone slab) discovered at Susa in 1901 and now preserved in the Louvre Museum in Paris. The laws were written on the slab in a writing known as cuneiform. The slab also has a fine piece of sculpture depicting Samas, the god of justice, looking into the eyes of King Hammurabi as if to inspire him.

Babylonian society was divided into three distinct classes: the patricians, the plebeians, and the slaves. Justice depended on the class to which a person belonged. For example, an article in Hammurabi's legal code said: 'If a patrician takes the eye of another patrician, one of his eyes also shall be taken. If he breaks the bone of another patrician, one of his bones too shall be broken.'

If, however, the person hurt was a plebeian, matters were different. The law said: 'If a patrician takes the eye or breaks a bone of a plebeian, he will pay a mine of silver.' Of course, the penalty was smaller if a slave was involved.

These laws seem very unfair to us today but the penalties inflicted are midway between the brutality of the Assyrian laws and the comparative leniency of the Hittites. We must remember that in the social conditions of Hammurabi's day such laws were needed to curb the vices and passions of the Babylonians.

Hammurabi died but his dynasty, or family, continued to rule for another 150 years although it never reached the same peak of glory as it had in his day.

How the people of Assyria and Babylonia wrote

The people of Mesopotamia, that is the Sumerians, Babylonians and Assyrians, created a system of writing that was quite different from that used in Egypt. The difference was because the people of Mesopotamia used clay to write on instead of papyrus as in Egypt.

It is difficult to make curved lines on clay with a stylus so the Mesopotamians invented a handwriting based on straight lines that resembled nails or wedges. For this reason, their handwriting was known as 'cuneiform', a word meaning 'wedge-shaped'. Cuneiform was later used on other materials, such as stone or metal. This writing was ideographic, as in Egypt, and used pictures instead of words.

How the Carthaginians practised trade

The Carthaginians had the reputation of being dishonest and thieving but this does not seem to be borne out by accounts written by Herodotus, the ancient historian. According to him, the Carthaginians would leave their goods on the seashore along the coast of Africa and would then retire to their ships and wait until the natives came along to inspect the goods. The natives looked at the goods and left a quantity of gold behind. The Carthaginians would then gather up the gold and value it. If they did not think it was enough, they would leave it there and withdraw again. Then the natives would come back and add more gold. If this was enough the Carthaginians would take it away and leave the goods behind.

How the old legends about trees were born

The story is well known of how Philemon and Baucis after showing warm hospitality to Jove and Mercury asked as a reward to be allowed to die together. Long after, they ended their lives at the same moment and were changed into an oak and a lime tree.

The daughters of the Sun watched as their brother, Phaethon, drove the carriage belonging to his father the Sun along the roads of the sky. They saw how, unable to control the horses, Phaethon went too near the earth almost scorching it. They wept when a thunderbolt from Jove struck Phaethon and their tear-drops fell and turned into amber and the sisters themselves into poplar trees.

The child Cyparissus loved a stag which had golden antlers and a silver ornament on its brow. One hot summer afternoon while the stag rested, the boy mistook it for an ordinary animal and killed it. When he saw what he had done he could not stop weeping and Apollo turned him into a cypress tree.

Jove

How the ancient peoples worshipped trees

In ancient times our ancestors believed that all nature was ruled by some mysterious but impersonal force which lay inside trees of a certain shape. This belief gave rise to many customs. The Romans would hang laurel branches outside their doors every year on the first day of March. The Germans raised birch maypoles in their villages. All these customs were designed to honour and display the mysterious governing force. The dead were buried near trees in the belief that they would be nourished by the life of the plant and their souls live longer.

As time went by the idea of an impersonal force was replaced by the belief that a divine being actually lived inside trees. For this reason forests became sacred places and temples were built near them.

The belief that spirits dwelt in trees was worldwide. The early Buddhists held that spirits could reside in trees and this is still believed in modern India. In

Juno

How the ancient Romans practised their religion

In the social and political life of ancient Rome no important action was taken unless the gods were first consulted. War was not declared, a building was not opened nor a magistrate appointed unless certain sacrifices had first been

The Temple of Vesta

ancient Rome the woodsman had to propitiate the gods before thinning a grove.

The ancient Egyptians thought the sycamore and the palm to be sacred. The sycamore grew almost miraculously at the limits of cultivated land where the barren sands of the desert began. The palm was venerated because it raised its beautiful head of fronds to the sky. Offerings of fresh fruit and cool water were made to these trees.

The oracular oak of Dodona in Greece was tended by priests who slept on the ground.

offered to the gods and the gods had found these acceptable.

Rome had numerous temples, many of them near the Forum, and the link between ordinary life and religion was very close. Temples sometimes acted as government offices to keep money in: in the temple of Saturn the public treasury was stored together with documents and war regalia.

Other famous Roman temples included that of Jupiter Optimus Maximus, of Vesta, Juno, Castor and Pollux, Venus, Janus and the Pantheon, the temple dedicated to all the gods.

Anpu and Bata, two brother-gods
worshipped by the Egyptians

old people without teeth. Some mother, perhaps, thought she would try and mash them up into a softer form to give to her baby. In this way she produced a rough sort of flour and discovered how to grind flour from grain.

The women used barley or wheat flour to make small pancakes which they dried in the sun. They then learned how to place pancakes on top of hot stones or in the embers of a fire. They discovered that the dough was much nicer to eat when it had been toasted and this was how bread was born. The men who went hunting by now were taking along these rough pieces of bread with them.

The first good pictures of primitive baking come from the tombs of the ancient Egyptians. They show all stages of breadmaking, from the removal of grain from the granary, the grinding on stones and subsequent sifting, to the mixing and kneading of the dough and the baking of the bread in large pots.

Man also learned to till the soil better: he sowed wheat and cultivated it carefully. Later man learned to prepare the soil with a plough pulled by animals instead of scratching it with a stick, and so the grain grew even better.

How bread was first made

When primitive man came to know grain he valued it greatly because it could be kept even during winter, when food was usually scarce. But those little hard grains were no good to young children or to

How food was sweetened before the discovery of sugar

At the time of the ancient Greeks and Romans food was sweetened with honey and manna. Honey is produced by bees and manna, as the Bible relates, is a vegetable, sugary substance found under the bark of certain ash trees in warm regions. Manna is also the name of a sticky substance, or resin, given off by a type of tamarisk shrub when nibbled by insects.

Later man learned to cultivate sugar-cane in Persia. Alexander the Great came across it and this plant soon found its way to Greece and Rome. But sugar was still a great luxury. It was only around the year A.D. 1000 that the Arabs extended the cultivation of sugar-cane along the entire coastal zone of the Mediterranean. Sugar was then brought back to Europe by soldiers returning from the Crusades.

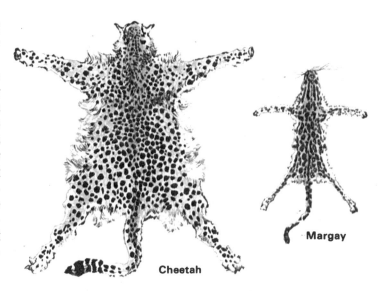

Cheetah

Margay

How the use of sugar spread

In China and especially in India the production of cane-sugar is ancient. Sugar was called *sarkara* in the ancient Sanskrit language. The Arabs turned this into *sucar*. The Greeks called it *saccaron* and today we have *sucre* in French, *zucchero* in Italian, *azucar* in Spanish and *sakhar* in Russian.

The Egyptians during the Middle Ages had already developed a sugar industry. But the real story of this product begins with the introduction of the sugar-cane to America after the discovery of that continent in 1492. Christopher Columbus took the first specimen plants over from the Canary Islands to the Antilles in the West Indies where the plant found perfect conditions for growth.

To extract the sugar the cane had to be crushed between iron rollers. The juice was heated several times and refined by adding lime to it. It was then passed from pan to pan and boiled until it turned into a sort of paste. This paste was then cooled in cone-shaped vats.

How primitive man protected himself from the cold

Primitive man had to keep warm when the Ice Age began to grip the world and the great ice sheets formed large regions of Europe and Asia. During the Palaeolithic or the Old Stone Age there were major changes in the climate of the world, which led to glaciation. This word gives us an idea of what happened. Huge, thick rivers of ice came down from the mountains and thrust their way into valleys. The ice moved south-

A Mousterian scraping hide with his carefully made tool

135

wards to zones which normally had a mild climate. The last of the great Ice Ages occurred when the first men appeared on the planet.

One of the major problems these primitive people had to face was the bitter cold in addition to the daily task of finding food. It was by hunting for his food that man protected himself against the cold for often the animals which he killed had soft, warm fur. The most common animals of the time were the wild horses and cattle, elephants, rhinoceroses, moose, bison and the woolly mammoth. There were also several kinds of cat, some of them of lion size.

Unfortunately the skins of these animals soon went bad and lost their fur. Man then learned that to make the skins last he had to scrape them very carefully and tan them.

The tools of this period include stone axes and flints. The flints were used, among other things, to scrape the skins and were among the highly valued tools of any early family.

How man learned to cook his food

When man discovered fire he acquired a mighty new weapon for he could defend himself better against animals which were terrified of this strange light that gave off heat. Man was also able to fight against the cold, light up the darkness and cook his food.

Man had always known that animals were afraid of fire, much more afraid than he was. He deduced from this that he could defend himself from even the fiercest beasts with fire. So he began to put burning torches at the entrance to his cave dwelling. These torches were kept burning throughout the night.

Until that time man had fed on raw meat. He probably first tasted cooked meat when a forest fire had trapped animals and burned them to death. He then learned that meat cooked by fire was more tender and manageable to eat as well as being tastier and easier to digest. In this way cooking by fire gradually spread from tribe to tribe.

Cup of Tutmosis III. About 1450 B.C.

136

How people ate in ancient times

Some centuries ago there were certain rules about eating food that amounted to religious laws. These laws applied to people like Moslems who were forbidden alcoholic beverages and pork. The Jews were also forbidden to eat pork and the meat of certain other animals. Many Moslems and Jews still observe these rules strictly as part of their religious traditions.

In Europe, when the early inhabitants stopped being wandering shepherds and settled down to farming, men began to eat more grain foods. At first they used spelt, an inferior form of wheat still grown in mountain regions of Europe. From this they made porridge-like meals and it was not for several centuries that farmers began to grow a better-quality wheat with which to make bread.

Other foods in those days included pickled olives, hard cheese and eggs.

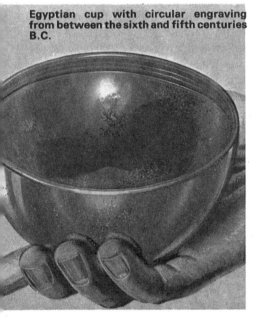

Egyptian cup with circular engraving from between the sixth and fifth centuries B.C.

How the adventure-seeking Phoenicians became rich

The ancient Phoenicians took to the seas to practise what they could do best: trade. Their position at a junction of both land and sea routes, under the protection of Egypt, favoured such activity, and they established a whole network of trading stations and colonies in the Mediterranean and beyond.

They traded in everything: metals such as silver from Spain and tin from distant Britain, pottery, cloth, silks from China, spices from Asia, ivory from Africa, perfumes from Arabia and papyruses from Egypt. The Phoenicians invented two important products: glass and the famous Tyrian purple dye made from the murex, a sea mollusc. The dye produced a beautiful, deep, red colour in clothes which every dandy in the Mediterranean region wanted to wear.

The Phoenicians were the first to introduce eastern spices to Europe. These spices were later to prove extremely important in world trade.

How the Colosseum looked when it was first built

The biggest building ever erected in ancient Rome was the Colosseum, originally named the Flavian amphitheatre. It was built by the emperors Vespasian, Titus and Domitian (A.D. 69–81) on the site of Nero's Golden House.

It was an enormous oval-shaped building about 185 metres long, 156 metres wide and 50 metres high. The outer wall had eighty doorways and was composed of three levels. On the upper level there were special brackets so that awnings could be fitted to shade the spectators from the Sun.

The Colosseum could hold more than 50,000 people. The spectators entered the building through the arched entrances on the ground floor which were all numbered. The places on the terraces depended on the social scale. The imperial and aristocratic families sat on the lower tiers near the arena; the higher the place in the amphitheatre the lower the social class.

In the vast arena gladiators armed with swords or nets and tridents fought one another, sometimes to the death, and there were also fights between men and wild animals. Some of the spectacles were extremely cruel and bloody.

How the first human communities were formed

When the great ice sheets that covered much of the land began to retreat northwards and the climate became warmer, man was able to come out of his cave dwellings and build huts above the ground. As the ice melted it gave rise to streams and rivers. There were also new lakes to be explored. All these waters were teeming with animal life such as fish and fowl which provided a ready supply of food.

Once the ice had gone, dense forests of willow and birch sprang up. Thousands of different kinds of birds lived in the branches and they were an easy target for man to shoot down with his bow and arrow. There was a whole new world to explore.

Man became a woodsman, a fisherman and a wildfowler. This new life had a great influence on social relationships between people. To get the best results possible from hunting and other forms of human activity, people came together in groups and formed the first tribes. These communities then became larger as life grew more complex. It became evident that people had to live and work together as a group to carry out all the operations necessary for living.

The basic nucleus of this community was the family. There was never a lack of work for the various members of the tribe. There were trees to be felled, huts to be built or repaired, fishing nets to be made from cords obtained from dried plant fibres. The work of women was more concerned with the home. They made rugs out of tree-bark to make their homes more comfortable; they made clothes of skin, sewn with bone needles; they cleaned and gutted the fish the men caught in abundance and dried it in the Sun; they cooked meals, gathered the fruits of the earth and prepared food stores for the winter.

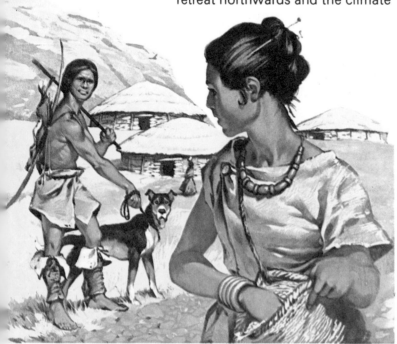

How cave-man buried his dead

In prehistoric times man buried his dead near where he lived. The deceased's possessions that he had used most frequently during his life, such as his axe and knife, were buried with him and enough food was placed beside his body to see him through to the next world. This suggests that man believed in a continued life after death.

Towards the end of the Stone Age it became the practice to bury the dead in caves which were not inhabited. These caves were sealed off with boulders to assure the deceased undisturbed peace. Collective burial grounds date from this period. These were the first graveyards and they were treated with great respect. The appearance of these cemeteries was a sign of an important social change and the development of religion.

How primitive man developed his religious beliefs

Primitive man had to face endless dangers in the hostile world he lived in. His enemies included the weather and the forces of nature all around him. In the midst of all this insecurity and concern for his survival, primitive man sought the help of superhuman beings and higher powers than himself.

The most frequently invoked were the forces of nature: fire, the Sun, light and darkness, thunder and lightning and the life-giving power of nature. When man was frightened he turned to these elements trustingly: at times it seemed better to him to call these forces by name than to use his weapons.

One man in the tribe was needed to supervise the worship of these forces of nature. This man was usually the most experienced of the tribe and he was appointed the priest, witch doctor or magician, responsible for a number of delicate and solemn tasks to do with life and death. He had to propitiate or please the gods by calling on them and offering them sacrifices, and he had to find the causes of illnesses, the curative properties of herbs and liniments. The witch doctor was aware of his own importance and power but as he was responsible to the whole community he always worked for the benefit of all.

The witch doctor was also responsible for teaching the young. He was the source of all the sacred traditions and the guardian of the tribe's cultural heritage and thus was the best qualified to prepare the younger generation to face life.

How Inca society was organized

Inca civilization reached its greatest splendour in the twelfth and thirteenth centuries when its society was based on feudalism. The supreme ruler was the *Inca*, or emperor, who was divine and worshipped by his subjects as the child of the Sun. The emperor was aided by a hierarchy of remote and isolated lawmakers who formed a social class of their own.

The Inca was the absolute ruler and guardian of all the state's possessions. He divided this wealth into three parts: one part he dedicated to the Sun-god and thus to the priests; the second part he took for himself and his court; and the third part he handed over to the community at large known as the *ayllu*.

The only people who were not obliged to work on the land were the members of the nobility. All others had to till the land for a good part of the year so that practically every man was a farmer producing his own food and clothing.

The work in the fields was extremely hard as the Inca kingdom was situated mainly on a high plateau about 3,000 metres above sea-level. Farmers had to build step-like areas known as terraces to grow maize, beans, tomatoes, chillis, peppers and cotton. They had few tools and had never discovered the use of the wheel, so that their working conditions were very tiring.

How the Mayas compiled their calendar

The Mayas were skilful astronomers and through their knowledge of the heavens were able to

The Incas of Pisac in South America had to build these terraces in order to grow crops in mountainous areas

Tiahuanaco, south-east of Lake Titicaca, where the oldest of the Inca civilizations once flourished

draw up a calendar. This was a great achievement at a time when there were practically no scientific instruments to help them.

The year *(tun)* was divided into eighteen periods *(vinal)*. The names of these eighteen periods were of various animals and colours. When the *vinal* added up to only 360 days, a special short *vinal* of only five days, known as 'ghosts', was added to complete the year. These five days were considered unlucky and nothing was ever done while they lasted.

In addition to this calendar there was a 260-day sacred almanac which was of supreme importance as a guide to daily conduct and an instrument for divining lucky days.

How the Aztecs justified their practice of human sacrifices

The Sun had a special place among the ranks of the Aztec gods; according to mythology it had been brought to life by the blood of all the other gods. This divine sacrifice served as an example to man and human sacrifices were an element of the ancient Aztec religion. The Aztecs believed that life could be continued only through death.

Often these human sacrifices became terrible blood-baths. Some 20,000 prisoners of war were slaughtered at the inauguration of the temple at Tenochtitlan.

How the ancient civilization of Zimbabwe was discovered

Zimbabwe, meaning 'stone house', refers to a huge collection of ruins of extremely ancient stone buildings. These buildings were situated

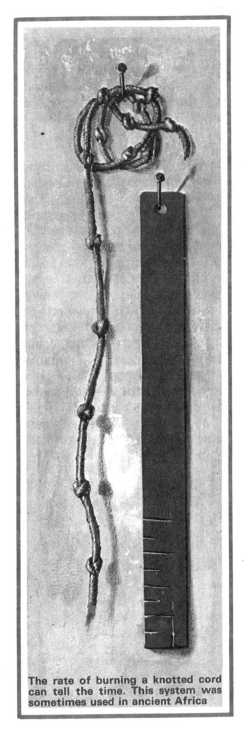

The rate of burning a knotted cord can tell the time. This system was sometimes used in ancient Africa

at the top of a granite hill that rose some 100 metres above the wild plain north of the river Limpopo which flows between Zimbabwe and South Africa. The ruins were discovered by chance by an

American hunter who had heard missionaries talk about them. The German anthropologist Carl Mauch was the first man to write about the ruins after organizing an expedition in 1871. Mauch worked on the account given to him by an African chief in a German mission.

When Mauch was abandoned by his porters he was helped by the Karanga tribe and as a guest of these people he was able to explore the region. He was convinced when he saw the colossal stone buildings and listened to all the old local legends that he had found the realm of the Queen of Sheba, which provided the gold for the temple of Solomon. Rumours soon spread that a great treasure lay hidden at Zimbabwe and much clandestine digging damaged the site before the authorities could act to stop it.

The majority of the objects excavated were locally made: pottery, iron tools and weapons, gold objects and carvings of human figures, birds and bowls in a local stone. A number of imported goods were also found including many varieties of glass beads.

Today we know that Zimbabwe was inhabited around 1000 B.C. and was only one of about 200 such centres scattered through the country called Zimbabwe.

How the slave trade was conducted

The hardest blow against the civilized societies of black Africa was the slave trade. It is impossible to say just how many men, women and children were dragged away from their villages in chains to distant lands. According to one authoritative source at least 9 million people were uprooted from their homes before 1776 and taken mainly to America.

A recent American investigation considered this figure too low. At least one million slaves died during the ocean crossings which were carried out in dreadful conditions.

A British doctor who served on board one of these slave ships gives some sort of idea of how terrible they must have been. This doctor said the slaves were stowed in the deepest hold of the ship and crammed together, without even enough room to stand up or stretch out. They were kept in chains which shackled their right hand and their left foot for the whole journey which sometimes lasted for months.

The doctor also remarked that it was impossible for a white man to spend more than a few minutes in these slave holds without fainting.

A slave caravan

How the people of Zimbabwe lived

Who were the first inhabitants of Zimbabwe? They were almost certainly Bushmen who were conquered during the Iron Age by a group of people who invaded their land. The newcomers tilled the soil and raised animals. They grew millet, sorghum and vegetables. Crops were cultivated on hillsides which were terraced into steps. These people also knew how to irrigate their land.

The greatest wealth came from the mines. To follow the gold veins in the rock that ran underground, narrow tunnels had to be dug. Women and children were used for this work because they could go down such narrow passages. There must have been many collapses and landfalls because many skeletons have been found some 8 metres underground. The gold was beaten from the rock with stone hammers or wedges and taken to the nearest stream. The rock was first heated and then plunged into the cold water so that it would break.

The first to exploit the gold trade were the Shona who came to the region in the tenth or eleventh century and established themselves there as rulers. The hill of Zimbabwe became a ritual centre. Many kings were buried there after the seat of government was transferred to the valley below. The most sacred place was the eastern enclosure. Here there was a cave with an unusual echo that was used cleverly by the witch doctors. The people gathered there to pray.

Zimbabwe continued to be occupied for some centuries until it was destroyed, probably during the 1830s or 1840s.

The mysterious stone buildings of Zimbabwe

Extensive mining and trading of metals occurred throughout Africa at the time of the exploration of the continent

143

THE HOW OF MAN

How the American Indians came to know the horse

The Indians who lived in North America had been hunters since time immemorial. They were used to wandering across the vast prairies in pursuit of wild animals. But these Indians only became really nomadic after the coming of the Europeans.

We have often seen on western films how the Indians galloped along bareback on their horses, so it is quite surprising to learn that before the Europeans came in the fifteenth century, no horses had existed in the New World. The horse revolutionized the life of the Indians and changed their ways greatly.

Horses were brought to America by the Spanish conquerors and settlers. Some of these animals escaped and began to breed in the wild, multiplying into the numerous herds of the prairies and pampas. Soon there were tens of thousands of them throughout the continent. The Indians caught and tamed them and then learned to ride them. It was then that life changed for the Indians. This horse, known as the mustang, brought enormous advantages: the Indian tribes could now move more easily from place to place and hunting became more effective and profitable.

How the Indians sent smoke signals

The American Indians used to pass on news from one tribe to another over great distances by using smoke clouds. This system was developed as a result of the vastness of the prairie, the flatness of which also helped to make the smoke visible from far off. There was a code of signals which consisted of a combination of long and short puffs of smoke. But smoke clouds were not the only means of communication among the American Indians. Sometimes they used lights flashed from mirrors reflecting the Sun. The Indians also had a system of writing using ideographs or pictures that resembled the ancient Egyptian hieroglyphs.

Victorio, an Apache Indian chief who sowed terror in the south-west around 1880

Sound did not play a major part in the Indian system of communication as it did in the tom-tom system of drumming in Africa. The Indians, however, imitated animal sounds at night to recognize friend from foe.

How the wandering Indians lived

The typical dwelling of the American Indian was the tepee. This was a cone-shaped tent usually made of animal skins stretched over a strong wooden framework based on a three- or four-pole foundation supporting other poles. A hole was left at the top of the tepee to let the smoke out. During the summer hunt tepees were pitched in a large circle, each family in its allotted place.

Another type of Indian house was the wigwam, a kind of domed hut with a frame of flexible poles covered in skins, mats or bark, which was not as comfortable as a tepee and was usually erected in the hunting grounds. The shape of the wigwam varied according to the region.

The tents and the implements of the Indians were made in such a way that they could be carried from place to place easily as the tribe went on its wanderings.

How the Indians spent the winter

The winter was by far the worst time of the year for the Indians. During this season food often became scarce, especially the herds of bison that wandered in the prairies in summer.

Many tribes would therefore split up and each section would go off on its own. Indians usually spent the winter near forests and rivers: the forests supplied firewood and the rivers, some of which were frozen, contained plenty of fish which was an easy food to catch.

The Indians were very skilful at catching large fish even with their bows and arrows. They could often catch and dry enough fish to last from one season to the next, and if not, some species of salmon could be caught at most times of the year. They preserved much of their meat by smoking it in the same way as bacon, but these smoked supplies often ran out before the end of the winter and then fish became valuable.

In winter the Indians also hunted small game animals. A variety of nooses, snares, traps and pitfalls were used and the peculiarities of the animal to be caught were carefully studied.

Indians used their bows and arrows to catch fish

Pre-Columbian peoples

How Pueblo villages are built

In the more remote and isolated valleys of the Rocky Mountains, in the south-west of the United States and in northern Mexico live the last descendants of the Pueblo Indians. The Pueblos are a peaceful but proud people, devoted to farming and the crafts, especially pottery and weaving. Their civilization reached its greatest peak in about the thirteenth century.

The Pueblo Indians are called after their villages (*pueblo* is the Spanish word for town). In about 1300 they moved south in search of more secure farmlands along the Rio Grande. They built their villages and created the way of life they had lived previously.

The Pueblo villages were built in two different positions: the first type was carved out of the rock of mountain-sides; the second was built in the valley, shaped as a semi-circular citadel or fortress. The cliff dwellings were the more impressive, built as they were out of the solid mountain rock. They often had three or four storeys built in stepped-back fashion so that the roofs of the lower rooms served as verandahs for the rooms above. They were communal buildings, usually quite small, consisting of between one and fifteen domestic rooms, with one or two ceremonial rooms. The lower inner rooms were used mainly for storing crops, while the upper rooms were for sleeping and living and also for the grinding of corn. They were reached by ladders or, occasionally, by staircases. The Indians built their villages in such remote places, which were uncomfortable and often far from water, for defensive reasons.

The Pueblo villages built in the valleys were more like the towns and villages we live in today.

How the Mexican Indians obtained alcoholic drinks

The Yuma, Pima and Papago were tribes of American Indians who lived mainly by farming, growing maize, beans and a kind of gourd

called squash. They were so skilful at their work that they had learned to irrigate their fields during the dry season and since A.D. 1 had used flood water for this purpose. Their society was based on the clan system.

One of their main feasts was the annual ceremony celebrating the ripening of the giant cactus (saguaro) and the coming of the summer rains. During this feast the people drank a beverage made from the fermented juice of cactus fruit. The beverage was very potent and those who drank it soon became intoxicated.

The saguaro ceremony had a magical significance, the beverage representing rain soaked in the soil.

How women were treated in Pueblo society

The Pueblo Indians lived in a matriarchal society which meant that the woman was honoured and was the true ruler. The clans, or family groups, were based on descent through the mother and not through the father. Property therefore belonged to the women and when they died they left it to their daughters. The farmland was also the undisputed property of the women.

When a man married he went to live in his wife's house. If his wife had no home, the husband had to build her one.

This structure of society, however, did not mean that men were the victims of the whims of the women and that they had no rights of their own. They were respected for their working skills and also for their contribution to the wealth of the whole Pueblo community.

How the Pueblos obtained water

Pueblos lived in arid regions and water was one of the most precious of their commodities. The Pueblos regarded rainfall as a sign of benevolence on the part of the gods. When it rained, the people in the villages, especially the children, would roll around in the muddy puddles in sheer joy. Villages usually had a large hollow scooped out in the rock or in the ground to hold water for as long as possible. The strictest of the Pueblo laws were those that governed the use of water during the dry season. When water supplies ran out the men of the village travelled to distant springs to obtain new supplies. Even the dew that appeared on plants during the night was gathered.

Drought in these regions could be very prolonged. Examination of tree rings has shown that one such period existed from 1276 to 1299.

How the people of the oases cultivate dates

Oases occur in the desert wherever there is a permanent supply of fresh water. They vary in size from a few acres round a stream to vast areas of naturally watered or irrigated land. The houses in the oases are built of clay and look like white cubes among the date palms which are the most important plants of desert oases. The desert people, known as the Tuareg, believe that the date palm should have its head in fire and its feet in water. For this reason farmers have built a system of underground canals in oases to bring water to the tree's roots.

Where there are no such irrigation canals date palms are cultivated together in the middle of a large circular ditch. This ditch can be up to 10 metres deep in order to reach the water under ground. Sand keeps sliding down the sides of the ditch and this has to be removed all the time to prevent the trees from being suffocated. In the past all the hard work needed to cultivate the date palm was sometimes in vain because enemies might raid the oases and steal all the fruit. To prevent this the farmers in the oases would strike up a rough bargain with the Tuareg tribesmen. Under this bargain the farmers supplied the fierce nomads with dates and grain in exchange for protection against raiders and thieves. This arrangement was known as *debiha*. One of the requirements was a curfew which meant that everybody in the oasis had to stay indoors after dark. Only the watchman appointed under the *debiha* was allowed to stay outside and patrol the neighbourhood. The watchman was always a Tuareg.

How the long houses of the Dayaks in Borneo are made

The Dayaks of Borneo, better known as head-hunters, make their home in the mountains that lie in the middle of the island which consists mainly of dense tropical forests. The word *dayak* or, more precisely *orang dayak*, means 'man of the interior'. The name is used to describe all the primitive peoples of Borneo.

The Dayaks have earned themselves a sinister reputation because of their savage ways but they have a strong sense of family ties and tribal relationships. For this reason they live together in long-house communities of several hundred people. In northern Borneo these houses are sometimes more than 200 metres long.

These large houses are designed to accommodate a whole clan the members of which live together collectively instead of being split up into families, each with its separate house. A single dwelling can house all the people in a village, or a community may have two or three houses.

Many Dayaks build their homes high above the ground on hardwood piles. These houses serve two purposes: defence against attacks from enemies and protection from the marshy ground below and frequent flooding from the rivers when they overflow in the rainy season.

Although they vary in size and internal arrangement, the Dayak houses are very simple structures, built of wood and covered in reeds. The front of the house has a large verandah, where everyone can gather, and there are inner family compartments. Entrance to the house is by a log or bamboo ladder.

How the Pygmies set their traps

The Pygmies who live in the dense forests of equatorial Africa are the smallest people on earth. A fully grown Pygmy man never grows to more than about 1·40 metres and a Pygmy woman reaches a height of about 1·35 metres. The forests provide their basic needs of food, water, firewood and clothing. Their huts are made by covering a beehive-shaped frame with leaves. They live in a camp for about a month and then abandon it and move on.

Pygmies are a very tough people and they are more than a match for even large animals. They make the best jungle explorers, beaters and hunters of Africa and their profound knowledge of the ways of all the animals they hunt enables them to make very clever traps to catch them.

Around their villages and in the forest the Pygmies dig deep pits in the ground. They cover the pits with twigs and branches and then with a layer of green leaves. They next place some dead leaves, moss, turfs and even termite hills to make the spot look like solid ground.

Only the Pygmy can recognize these almost invisible traps: even a cunning animal like the leopard fails to see them. The big animals of the forest are often the victims of these traps. These include elephants, buffaloes and hippopotamuses which the Pygmies could not hope to catch by any other method.

As soon as an animal falls into the trap the Pygmies rush up and kill it with their spears. The meat on the animal is shared out and eaten immediately.

How to recognize a person who chews betel nuts

Betel nuts could be described as the chewing-gum of the East. They are the fruit of the areca or betel palm, a tree originally from the Sunda Islands which grows to about 15 metres. The fruit are prepared by boiling in water, cutting up into slices and drying in the Sun. In Malaysia where more than 5 million people chew betel nuts, the nut is treated with lime, nutmeg and other substances. If the nut is kept inside the mouth when chewed, without being swallowed, it causes a lot of saliva to be produced so that the person chewing has to spit a great deal.

The betel nut stains the teeth a dark reddish-brown. The lips and gums are also stained this colour and it is easy to recognize anyone who chews it. Betel juice is a stimulant and creates a faint feeling of intoxication.

How the Polynesians drive away ghosts

The Polynesians believe that the souls of the dead, before they find their way to paradise, wander to and fro playing unpleasant tricks on the living. In spite of the teachings of Christianity the Polynesians are very much afraid of the *tupapau*, as they call these ghosts, and believe that they heavily out-number the living people.

For this reason few Polynesians will go out alone at night, even with a lantern, and no Polynesian will sleep without a light by his bed. Throughout the islands of Polynesia there are specially furnished houses for the ghosts to meet.

According to the Polynesians most of the ghosts simply make a lot of noise by chattering away to one another. Some *tupapau*, however, are thought to be dangerous. These ghosts can cause illnesses and assume the strangest of shapes. The Polynesians believe they are protected from the *tupapau* by spirits called *varua-ino*. These spirits are evil and they come to life whenever a comet is seen in the skies. At such times the *varua-ino*, who are the sworn enemies of the *tupapau*, attack and destroy the ghosts.

Polynesians have learned to live with these ghosts and to keep them at bay by flailing the air with a bamboo pole from time to time and by calling the name of a *varua-ino* to come to their aid. This is enough to drive any mischievous ghost away.

Ornamental mask from the Caroline Islands

Maori sculpture

A wood carving done by the head-hunters of New Guinea

Polynesian sculpture from Rarotonga

Easter Island sculpture

How the Polynesians practise their religion

In Tonga, one of the island groups of Polynesia, there is a legend which has a striking similarity to the story of Cain and Abel in the Bible. Tangaroa, the fisherman-god, one day threw his fishing line badly and his hook caught the ocean bed. Tangaroa pulled and tugged with all his might and main and brought to the surface a number of islands which included Tonga.

The islands were deserted and the god felt lonely so he said to his sons: 'Take your wives and make your home in Tonga.' The two sons obeyed their father and shared out the island between them. Yaka-Ako-Ouli, the younger brother, was a hard working man who knew how to make axes and necklaces. Tubo, the elder brother, was an idler. He was filled with envy against his brother and one day he killed him.

Tangaroa immediately cursed Tubo and all his children. He summoned the family of the dead man and told them: 'Sail out to sea in your canoes and go to the islands in the east. Your skin will be as white as your soul but the children of Tubo will have a black skin.'

So, according to the Polynesians, Tangaroa populated the islands of the Pacific and much of the world with both good and bad people.

How the Polynesians build their huts

In Polynesia the construction of a house is accompanied by a ceremony that combines politics with religion. The building contract has to be drawn up with the *tafugas*, a guild of skilled craftsmen regarded as the guardians of the art of the god Tangaroa.

Once the contract has been agreed the whole village celebrates the erection of the main pole. This part of the house symbolizes the link between the world of mankind and that of the gods. The rafters of the house are fixed to the main pole and to the poles that form the outer sections of the house. The dome-shaped roof is then placed on this framework.

Polynesians use no precision instruments and do all the building by eye. Their accuracy is amazing. Every house has an individual design reflecting the *tafugas* who built it. When the house is finished the *tafugas* puts his own special mark on the timber and the end of the job is celebrated by feasting.

How the Polynesians cook their native dishes

Taro is a staple food of Polynesia. It has been extensively cultivated for its large, spherical, underground tubers, rich in starch. It grows on open hillsides and when harvest time comes the various family clans leave the villages early in the morning, carrying baskets and knives. The villagers split up into groups. The men do the heavy work, such as pulling the taro out of the ground and lopping off its root and putting it into the baskets. Some of the stems of the plants are specially chosen and re-planted for future crops. The women cut the grass and leave it laid out to dry and become fertilizer for the soil.

During important feasts the job

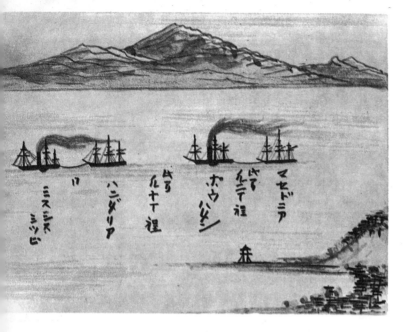

Above: Commodore Perry
Left: a Japanese print showing 'the black ships'

of cooking is left to the men of the tribe. The men prepare the ovens which consist of flat stones heated until they are red-hot. The food is cooked on these hot stones according to a traditional order of the menu: suckling pigs, vegetables, fish, turtles and breadfruit cut into four. The most expert of the cooks prepare the *poi*, a thin paste of taro starch wrapped in banana leaves. All the food is wrapped in leaves, served in wooden bowls or platters and eaten with the fingers.

The whole oven is covered in leaves and matting to keep the heat in.

How Japan became a modern country

Until July 1853 Japan had been a land closed to all contacts with the West. No ports were open to Western ships, missionaries who tried to convert the people to Christianity were killed and all forms of Western culture were banned. But time did not stand

still outside Japan. The early steamships that sailed across the Pacific Ocean needed places where they could replenish their fuel supplies and Japan was the ideal place for this. Despite much pressure from Western countries, however, Japan still remained closed to all their shipping.

The United States government then decided to send a squadron of naval ships under the command of Commodore Matthew C. Perry. Perry was told to persuade the Japanese to sign a treaty opening up some Japanese ports to Western ships. With two frigates and two sailing vessels he entered the fortified harbour of Uraga on 8 July 1853. He refused to obey Japanese orders to leave and demanded that a suitable person be sent to receive the documents he had brought. The Japanese finally complied.

Perry made a great impression on the Japanese dignitaries by his firm and dignified bearing. He returned with a larger force the following year and on 31 March 1854 the first treaty between the

United States and Japan was signed.

By this treaty shipwrecked seamen were promised better treatment and American ships were able to obtain fuel and supplies at two Japanese ports. Japan's traditional policy of isolation was broken and from that moment it established contact with the West. It was destined to become the leading country in the Far East and one of the world's great powers. Only some fifty years later it subjected the Russian fleet to a crushing defeat.

How Papuan canoes are built

In Papua and the surrounding islands the people still use a seagoing craft which is made of three or more canoes joined together by strong pieces of timber. The individual boats form a single vessel on which a strong bamboo deck is placed. There are two masts in the middle, very close to each other, and from these are hoisted rather strange looking sails that resemble the claws of a lobster.

The double canoe of Hawaii and the Tongan *calie* are examples of a twin-boomed craft. The Hawaian craft was first developed in the south seas and consists of two canoes of the same length. The canoes are joined together by curved pieces of timber which also support the single sail.

The Tongan *calie* is more complicated and interesting. The *calie* consists of two canoes of different length joined together by thick timber that supports a platform or deck. Apart from the main mast this deck also carries a sort of cabin large enough to take several persons. The *calie* was used both for fishing and carrying goods and passengers.

How bamboo wood is used

In the countries where bamboo grows this wood is used in an incredible number of ways as it is cheap and plentiful. Bamboo stems are used to build bridges, houses, boats, irrigation pipes and receptacles of all kinds. One of the best known uses of bamboo in its flexible state is in fishing rods. This wood is also used to make garden furniture because it is light and strong and stands up to the weather. The shoots of the bamboo are also delicious to eat.

Bamboo belongs to the graminaceous family of plants, which means it is a sort of grass. It has a rhizome, or root part, which grows from year to year and produces new stalks. Sometimes these stalks are enormous, growing to more than 30 metres high.

The stalks are hollow and jointed, with knots from which branches grow. These branches become covered in leaves and the bamboo resembles a tree. Most bamboos flower very rarely and are thornless, but a few kinds have sharp spines.

Hawaian double canoe

Japanese bamboo eel-trap

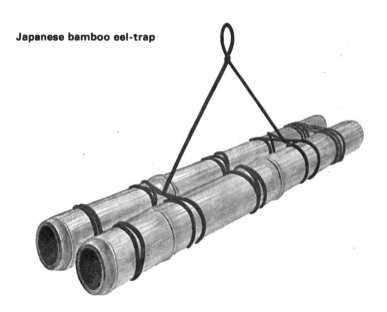

The search for food is the duty of every member of the Aborigine tribe although the tasks of the men differ from those of the women. The men do most of the hunting, mainly for kangaroos, emus and large lizards. Their weapons are spears and boomerangs, but to catch the emu they pound up pituri leaves with water as a bait, so that the bird becomes stupefied and is easily speared.

Sometimes the men are away from the encampment for several days on hunting trips. During these periods the women are responsible for feeding the tribe with whatever animal or vegetable food they can find.

How the Aborigines of Australia eat

The Aborigines of Australia have a rich and balanced diet. They not only eat meat, fruit, vegetables and even a type of bread but sometimes they supplement their calorie intake by eating giant ants and the big, fat grubs they find under the bark of trees. It is a rather startling sight to see the Aborigines eating these creatures, which they consider delicacies, while they are still alive and squirming.

How the *kuran* of the Aborigines of Australia behaves

The Aborigines of Australia believe in the existence of a life-force they call *kuran* which is present in every living thing. The intensity of this force varies in the different creatures which have it: the Aborigines believe, for example, that it is stronger in a man than in a woman, in an emu than in a wild turkey, that it is the same intensity in plants and weak in more simple forms of life. They believe that the life-force is at its most powerful in the medicine man or witch doctor, the 'clever fellow'.

The life-force does not cease to exist when an individual dies. In fact they believe that the force shows itself at its strongest at such times almost as if it were expressing its dislike of being excluded from physical life. The Aborigines do not believe that death is caused by natural causes such as illness, old age and accidents: to them death is always the work of an unfriendly

supernatural power.

As soon as a dead person has been buried the whole Aborigine village moves away from the grave so as not to be troubled by the *kuran* of the deceased. After about three months it is thought that the life-force will vacate the old body and be reincarnated in another.

How the Aborigines trick the kangaroo

The only domestic animal known to the Aborigines is the dingo, the Australian wild dog which is trained and bred by the Aborigines and helps them to hunt. For the primitive Aborigines hunting is often a real adventure, involving long journeys on foot through the desert, the use of primitive weapons and great difficulty because of the lack of any form of transport.

In the main the Aborigine hunts animals which move very swiftly and are difficult to catch. Some species of kangaroo can jump further than 9 metres and nearly 3 metres high, and travel at speeds of over 65 kilometres an hour.

There is one type of kangaroo which has a reddish-brown fur that makes it almost invisible against the surrounding countryside. This kangaroo can hear a suspicious noise several thousands of metres away and it can move very swiftly so that not even a dingo can catch it.

The Aborigines use their cunning to catch this animal. The marksmen take up their position along a kangaroo track. The other men then create a terrible din to frighten the animals which are killed by spears from the hidden marksmen.

How the Dayaks stretch their ears

It is a very common custom among the Dayaks of Borneo to wear heavy rings in their ears. The rings are made of iron or brass and are worn through the pierced lobes of the ears. The weight of the metal stretches the lobes which reach a length of several centimetres. To Western eyes these stretched earlobes look absolutely hideous but for the Dayaks it is a sign of beauty.

The Dayaks are a savage people but they care about elegance. They love headgear such as turbans, feather crowns and fur caps. All these play a part in tribal ceremonies and war celebrations when, to the music of copper gongs beaten by women, the men go through all the movements of combat.

Jewellery does not vary much between men and women. Both wear necklaces, ear-rings, bracelets and colourful hair-grips.

Man wearing a *burnus*

Tuareg

Kabylia

Berber nomad

Algerian costumes

How the Tuareg dress

The picturesque dress of the Tuareg people is also extremely functional because their voluminous clothes offer the best protection against the scorching heat of the desert Sun. The Tuareg wear two tunics made of light wool over trousers which are very broad and fastened round the ankles. These trousers give the Tuareg greater freedom of movement when they are riding. They also wear a broad leather belt designed to regulate the breathing during camel races.

The most important feature of the dress of these nomadic people is a band of dark-blue cloth slightly more than 3 metres long, which is light and looks like a veil. It is worn round the face as a mask, covering the mouth and nose, with a slit left for the eyes, and prevents sand and dust from harming the breathing passages.

The colour of this veil and of the clothes is not accidental. The blue offers protection against the rays of the Sun. To avoid bad sunburn the Tuareg keep rubbing their blue veils on any exposed skin. The blue dye stains the skin and that is why these nomads are also known as 'the blue people'.

How Bedouin tents are made

The wandering Bedouin who live in the Arabian peninsula live in black tents which are usually about 10 metres long and 4 metres wide. These tents consist of several strips of cloth sewn together which can be added to or reduced according to the needs of the family. The tent is pitched on three parallel lines of poles. Usually, one side is left open and it is always anchored firmly enough with taut ropes to stand up to the fiercest winds.

The material for the tent is thick and hard-wearing. It is woven by the women on rough looms from goat and camel hair.

Inside the tent the women's compartment is often divided off

by a shoulder-high screen. The side nearer the entrance is reserved for the men and for receiving guests. The part occupied by the head of the family has a fireplace and everything necessary for the ceremony of making and drinking coffee.

The furniture consists of cushions, rugs and leather pouffes. The most important item is a copper tray on a folding wooden table which is sometimes elaborately carved and decorated with inlaid ivory.

How dromedaries behave in the desert

The dromedary is the most precious piece of property that the desert nomad has but it is not an easy animal to handle. It never becomes friends with its masters or anybody else Every night, these animals have to be forced down to their knees on the ground and tethered firmly.

The dromedary is extremely strong. With one heave it can throw off all its load and gallop madly off, sweeping everything aside that lies in its path. To lead them the nomads use long reins tied to an iron ring driven through the right nostril of the animal.

Camels can flourish on thorny plants, leaves, twigs and dried grasses that other animals would refuse. When the feeding is good, they accumulate stores of fat in their humps which, in emergencies, they can use for sustenance and for the manufacture of water. They are thus able to fast and go without water for several days.

There is one variety of dromedary known as the *mehari* which is extremely swift and the Tuareg tribesmen often owe their lives to the speed of this light-coloured camel. All dromedaries are fast and they are used whenever a journey is a matter of life and death, when a well has to be reached before the water runs out or when an important prey has to be caught.

A nomad can carry in the roomy saddlebag of his *mehari* everything he needs for his lonely desert life: food, clothing, tobacco, salt and the leather containers for butter and tea.

Every Tuareg tribe owns large herds of these camels. The young animals graze by themselves near the camp. When the mothers come together to feed them with their milk, the camels are milked by the tribe's servants. Camel's milk is rich and frothy and is best drunk immediately because it curdles easily and clots if it is heated. The Tuareg drink considerable quantities of this milk.

Lapp costumes

How the Lapps protect themselves from the cold weather

The diet of the Lapp people is not very varied but it is rich in calories and helps these nomads to stand up to the rigours of their difficult climate.

Lapland is a region of northern Europe stretching across the north of Norway, Sweden, Finland and Russia from the Norwegian coast to the White Sea. The climate is dominated by winter: in some places, the Sun does not rise for six or seven weeks in winter, but stays continually in the sky for a corresponding period in summer. Rivers freeze in November and thaw in May, and snow depths vary greatly.

The staple food is reindeer meat and fish eaten fresh during the summer and dried or smoked in winter. The Lapps cook their food on fires lit by the women every day in the centre of the tent beneath a hole which acts as a chimney. Once the meal is over the fire is covered very carefully and the women wash the dishes and the dogs eat the left-overs. Lapps keep their tent-homes scrupulously clean.

Apart from their household tasks the women also make the leather clothing which Lapps wear summer and winter alike. In winter Lapps wear trousers made of reindeer-skin with the furry side turned inwards. In summer they discard these clothes for lighter ones in leather or rough cloth.

Lapps walk a great deal and shoes are an extremely important part of their dress. They wear soft boots, stuffed with grass which is changed frequently.

The holiday costume is covered in hand-embroidery and decorated with shawls, hoods and, for the men, with a cap the shape of which indicates to which tribe he belongs.

How reindeer migrate

In spring the Lapps leave behind the woodlands of the south where they spend the winter and set out for the pastures in the northern mountains. The Lapps move in small family groups, leading their herd of reindeer along established tracks which usually follow the courses of rivers. The rivers are still frozen and the Lapps use them as safe roads for their sledges, laden with provisions. The reindeer are used to following the same route and move along slowly, feeding as they travel.

Half-way through the journey, when spring breaks, the Lapps pitch their tents for a period lasting several weeks. It is at this time that the baby reindeer are born and the tribe has to wait until they are able to walk by themselves. The young reindeer do not take long to learn how to trot about and the herd moves on once more. The destination is the far north where the tundra, the 'cold desert' of northern Norway, Sweden, Finland and Iceland, ends and the Arctic Ocean begins. The reindeer herd spends the short summer on the grassy shores and on the islets along the coast before travelling south once more.

Lapps consume large quantities of reindeer milk and use it to make delicious cheese. When the icy north wind blows and the family is gathered together in the tent, the mother prepares a hot drink by dissolving chunks of reindeer cheese in hot water. This drink provides a great deal of energy and warmth.

Lapps have hunted reindeer since the earliest times and have kept small numbers, but breeding them in large herds is comparatively recent.

Costumes of certain countries of the Asian part of the Soviet Union

Siberia

Uzbekistan

Kirghizia

How the Kurds live in their encampments

The Kurds were once pure nomads, driving their flocks between the Mesopotamian plains and the highlands of Turkey and Iran, but today they prefer to live in one place for considerable periods.

A Kurd encampment, known as a *kissla*, usually consists of four or five tents. The tents are made of goatskin sewn together and held up by wooden poles. The site of the encampment is chosen by the sheikh or leader. Life in the encampments follows the rhythm of the daily tasks connected with the breeding of sheep and cattle.

The men come out of their tents early in the morning to take the animals to the grazing grounds which are located in nearby hollows. The animals are left there until the evening. During the day the men make leather goods which they sell to local markets. The women weave carpets with which to decorate their homes and cloth for their own use.

The main duty of the women is to milk the animals. From the milk they make, cheese, butter and yoghourt which, mixed with water, produces *ayran*, their main drink.

An Inca road in Peru with the Andes in the distance

How the Indians use llamas

The typical beast of burden in the Andes region of South America is the llama. These animals are mostly bred by the Indians for their milk and their thick wool. Usually white, the animals can vary in colour to solid black, with any combination of brown or black spots.

The llama is a stolid and tough animal, able to endure thirst and to exist on a wide variety of vegetation. It is often used to carry loads up steep mountain paths and in places where there are no roads, travelling slowly but safely even in the most difficult and dangerous places. It can carry a load of about 60 kilogrammes for about five days on end without resting. When overloaded or exhausted, however, it lies down, hisses, spits and kicks, refusing to move until relieved of some weight or adequately rested. Only the male llamas are used as beasts of burden. The females are kept in the grazing grounds, and although they do not yield very much milk the Indians put it to a number of uses. Llamas are also bred for their meat which resembles pork.

How the floating gardens of Lake Titicaca are made

The shores of Lake Titicaca which is situated amid the Andes mountains 3,812 metres above sea-level, are covered in vast stretches of reed beds. These plants provide the Indians with the raw material to build their boats and their floating gardens. These gardens are large rafts, rectangular in shape and made of reeds tied together. A layer of soil is placed on the rafts, furrowed according to an ancient tradition and then planted with vegetables. The result is a floating garden. The raft is then towed to a sheltered part of the lake shore where the vegetables can grow. The lake is very deep (about 370 metres) and so the water temperature remains quite constant. Due to the great altitude the plants do not grow as well as they would lower down.

Every so often these rafts are towed back to the shore, laden with ripe crops which are gathered and shared out by the Indian families.

The Indians also cultivate the area surrounding Lake Titicaca, planting potatoes, quinoa, barley and maize on terraced fields around the shores.

How *curare* is prepared in the forests of the Amazon

In the dense jungles of the river Amazon the Indians can immediately recognize the plants that contain the deadly poison known as *curare* which can kill within a few minutes.

The process of preparing this poison is one of the most sacred traditions of the tribe and carefully passed on from warrior to warrior. The Indians use a special knife to scrape the bark of certain trees. They then put a large pot on the fire and when the water comes to the boil they put in the bark scrapings. The water evaporates slowly until there remains a thick, dark and gummy paste, smelling like tar. This is the poison. Before it cools, the hunters dip their arrows in it and pour the rest into small flasks which they carry from their belts. Once the *curare* has dried it becomes extremely hard and has to be diluted.

How a man gets a wife in Kashmir

Kashmir is a large territory situated between Pakistan and India. It is rich in beautiful and picturesque valleys and high mountains. The inhabitants of this region are usually sturdy and robust. They have fine features with expressive and intelligent faces. The women of Kashmir are renowned for their beauty. They have a very sweet, and yet very wilful, character.

The Kashmiris have a particular custom regarding marriage. The young man cannot obtain the hand of his beloved before first 'earning' or 'deserving' her. He does this by working in the house of his future father-in-law. The poorer the young man is, the longer he has to work and quite often this service can last for several years.

Amazonian peoples

Mboyes

Charrua

Guarani

How the Piaroa Indians build their huts

Many Indians in the Amazon river basin live in collective or communal houses. One of the most functional examples is the large, cone-shaped, thatched hut used by the Piaroa Indians. To build one of these huts the Indians construct a framework made of long, thin poles. They work on these poles, perching like monkeys several metres above the ground. The poles are fixed to thicker poles which mark out an area of about 8 metres square.

The whole tribe takes part in the building work. Some weave flexible branches on to the framework while others place dried banana or palm branches on top of the structure. At the top of the conical roof, a hole is left as a chimney. At this point the Indians always place a twisted branch to frighten away evil spirits.

To keep harmful insects out of the communal hut the door is fitted with a type of screen. Light filters through a series of divisions in the roof which the Indians open up as the Sun moves across the sky.

These huts house from six to eight families. Each one has its own fireplace round which hammocks are hung one above the other. The duty of the woman is to keep the fire lit. A wooden platform near the ceiling acts as wood store and a place to stow away any possessions the Piaroa may have.

How manioc was born according to the legends

Manioc is a root which contains poison. But the Indians who live in the Amazon river basin have

tuber with wooden boards fitted with stone teeth, then squeeze the pulp and strain the juice through a filter made of plant materials. The pulp is washed several times and then shaped into large slabs which are put on the roof to dry in the Sun. When manioc is chewed and then left to ferment it produces an alcoholic beverage which is greatly enjoyed by the Indians.

How the Indians of Brazil paint their bodies

In many of the dense forests along the river Amazon man still lives as he did in prehistoric times. Driven even farther into the interior by the inroads of modern civilization, the Indians of Brazil have a hard struggle to maintain their simple ways of life.

During times of war or at certain ceremonies and feasts, these Indians paint their bodies with juices obtained from certain aromatic plants. The predominant colour is a bright red, obtained from the unucu and the onoto. The dark blue comes from the sap of the American juniper.

In some tribes the men cover their entire bodies in the most fantastic tattoos which are considered to have a magical power. In other tribes only the face is tattooed. The tattoos are done by methods and with ceremonies that vary from tribe to tribe.

There is a special tattoo given to young men when they reach the end of their initiation period which marks them out as having been accepted by their tribe. The ceremony of the Camayura Indians is called *omaruru* and consists of two dark blue rings under the eyes.

The Jivaro, who have a blind

found a way to make this plant edible and they have transformed it into their staple food.

The word 'manioc' comes from the Tupi Indian, meaning 'house of Mani'. The legend told by the Indians says that Mani was a fair-skinned, very beautiful little girl and the daughter of a chief. Mani died when she was one year old and the whole tribe came to mourn at the hut where she was buried. Then a strange plant began to grow from the child's grave. Birds which pecked and nibbled at the plant became intoxicated. One day the earth opened up to reveal the white tuber of the plant and the Tupi saw in this tuber the body of little Mani. They ate it and in this way learned how to use manioc.

The method of removing the poison from the tuber is very laborious and is a task left for the women to do. They scrape the

faith in the magical powers of tattoos, have invented a method carrying out the operation simply. This consists of a tattoo 'stamp' made of a piece of wood or clay on which the tattoo design has been carved or cut out.

How the name 'Eskimo' originated

The name 'Eskimo' comes from the language of the northern Red Indians and means 'a person who eats raw meat'. It is an appropriate name because the Eskimos live mainly by hunting and fishing and in winter do not always cook the animals they catch.

This is because it is impossible to find any fuel for a fire in the icy waste that they inhabit. The only form of fire they have is produced by burning the oil of seals or whales in shallow, saucer-shaped lamps, made from pottery or stone. These lamps are used primarily to give light but the Eskimos can also boil their meat and fish over them. These foods are also frozen or dried.

There is another reason why the Eskimos sometimes eat raw meat: in this way they get the greatest possible nourishment. The Eskimos make up for the lack of vitamins from vegetables by eating the kidneys and liver of their prey raw. These organs have an abundant store of all the vitamins needed by the human body.

How the Eskimos catch seals

Eskimos spend much of their time hunting seals. During the spring and summer they pursue the seals in their canoes, or kayaks, harpooning them in the open sea, but all sorts of cunning ruses are also used. The Eskimo disguises himself as a seal and lies motionless for hours waiting for one of the animals to come near him, or he will drag himself along like a seal to where a group of these animals are basking in the Sun.

The most unusual methods of hunting are used in winter when seals spend most of their time under the ice-covered water of the sea. Every seven or nine minutes they must come to the surface to

gulp down a new supply of air and for this purpose the seals open up holes in the ice as breathing places.

A skilful hunter first finds these breathing holes which are hidden under heaps of snow, and then waits motionless for hours until a passing seal decides to come up for air. When it does the Eskimo strikes with his harpoon.

The Eskimo uses every part of the seal: the skin, the fat, the meat and the bones. For example, the seal's flippers with the bones removed make good water bottles. The Eskimo hangs these water bottles near his chest under his clothes when travelling so that the contents will not freeze hard.

The skin is often used for clothes, especially for the outer shoe or boot because sealskin does not spoil with dampness.

How Eskimos count

The Eskimo counts on his fingers. The little finger on the left hand represents the number one. The same finger on the right hand represents six. When the Eskimo has run out of fingers he uses his toes. To say twenty the Eskimos have an expression which means 'a complete man', indicating that all the fingers and toes have been used.

How the Eskimos build their kayaks

During the short Arctic summer when the ice melts the Eskimos go sailing in small one-man canoes called kayaks. These are used for hunting. Umiaks, large open boats made of skins, are used for transport.

Walrus *(Odobenus rosmarus)* which inhabits the Arctic seas and is hunted by the Eskimos

Kayaks are a masterpiece of human ingenuity because they are often built without a single piece of wood being used.

A typical kayak has a framework made of round pieces of thin bone placed straight up and down. These form a support for a covering of sealskin that is sewn on. The stitching is waterproofed with fat also taken from the seal. The man sits in a round opening in the middle of the kayak and propels it with a paddle.

When the Eskimo sits in his kayak he stops up the round opening with his fur clothing to prevent the water seeping into the canoe if it should overturn. The kayak is so light and unstable that the slightest movement in the wrong direction or even a sudden gust of wind can capsize it. But it is also so light and manoeuvrable that the Eskimo can put it the right way up again immediately with a stroke of his paddle.

How edible birds' nests are gathered

The birds' nests which the Chinese use as an ingredient to make their famous birds' nest soup are built by a swift belonging to the group of birds known as *Collocalia*. This bird closely resembles the swallows of Europe.

Gathering birds' nests

These swifts are great fliers. They make their home on steep cliffs that rise out of the sea in the islands of eastern Asia. The birds build their nests among these rocks and two or three times a year the nests are gathered to be sold in Chinese markets.

The work of gathering these nests is quite dangerous because very steep cliffs have to be scaled to reach them. Once a colony of nests has been reached they can be removed quite easily. The shelf-like nests are made of the saliva of the birds, which goes hard rapidly. It is this saliva, softened by soaking and then cooking, that is used in making the delicious soups.

How the people of Taiwan live

Taiwan, which is also called Formosa, is the largest of the Chinese islands. It is separated from the mainland by a stretch of water called the Formosa Strait. The oval-shaped island has an area of 35,834 square kilometres. The sixty-six small islands that lie scattered about Taiwan are not much more than rocks in the ocean. Their combined area is only about 127 square kilometres.

Far inland, in the mountains of Taiwan, live a tribe of aborigine people descended from the first inhabitants of the island before the Chinese came. These tribes, numbering about 200,000, refuse to have any contact with modern civilization. They have a reputation for being fierce and some of them are thought to be cannibals. The aborigines often fight among themselves but their battles are more part of a religious attitude than a display of hatred for one another.

Before they go to battle these people free a bird which shows by the direction of its flight where the warriors must go. This ceremony shows there is no hatred for any particular enemy and the custom of fighting, regrettable as it may be, is pure ritual. It is through fighting that one group of aborigines asserts its right to live rather than another.

In this sense the ritual has a social significance as well as a religious one. Every member of the village takes part in the campaign against the enemy.

How the legend explains the origin of the Veddas of Sri Lanka

In some of the mountain regions of the centre and the east of Sri Lanka (formerly Ceylon), amid dense forests that make life difficult, lives a very ancient people who have found shelter in this wild region and continued their old way of life: the Veddas.

The way of life of the Veddas is thousands of years old. Little is known about their origin, but there is a verse chronicle written by Buddhist monks that tells part of the story. The chronicle is called the *Mahavamsa* ('Great History'). It relates that the first king of Sri Lanka was called Vijaya. The origins of this king are buried in legend but his existence is more or less certain. One story says he was the child of a princess and a lion. Vijaya's first wife ran away with the children to the mountains, and the Veddas were the descendants of those refugees.

This legend may be pure fantasy, but one theory is that the Veddas are a people who fled from the Aryans who invaded northern India in about 2000 B.C. and took refuge in the territory where they now live.

Today the Veddas have been largely absorbed into the population of Sri Lanka and have adopted its language. In 1911 they were reported to number about 5,300, but in 1964 the government of Sri Lanka listed their population at about 800. Since then, the Veddas have virtually died out.

Costumes of Sri Lanka

THE HOW OF DOMESTIC ANIMALS

How to bring up a little bird that has fallen from its nest

Quite often in spring newly born birds fall from the nest and lie helplessly on the ground. What can we do to aid these poor little creatures?

First of all they need a warm nest. A small box or basket stuffed with woollen rags is perfect for this. If the little bird is only a few days old it will have to be kept warm. This can be done by keeping a 25-watt bulb alight over the box. The bulb should be shaded so that the light does not distress the bird. The box is best kept in a quiet corner, preferably in sub-dued light, and away from draughts and gas fumes. It must be placed well out of the reach of domestic pets.

The biggest problem is how to feed the fledgling. If it gets the wrong food it will die. A young bird also has to have certain quan-tities of food given to it at certain intervals. In normal conditions nestlings are fed about every ten minutes by their parents. If they go for more than one hour without food they begin to be ill.

As to the kind of food, birds normally eat insects, grubs and worms. They enjoy maggots but they will also take flies. Use a pair of tweezers with rounded ends to feed the bird.

How to stop kittens from scratching the furniture

It is quite easy to stop kittens from scratching the walls or the furni-ture. They do this for exercise and to sharpen their claws, rather as we file our nails. The cat has to keep trimming its nails or they become too long and that is why it scratches wooden objects such as the furniture, trees and wooden fences.

Many cats are given special scratching posts, a block of wood or an old box. They soon learn to sharpen their claws on these and to leave the furniture unmolested.

How to wean kittens

To wean kittens away from their mother's milk, add the beaten yolk of an egg to some milk or a few spoonfuls of broth which is not too salty, and some honey or sugar. Another method is to use boiled rice and put it in the kitten's milk or broth with some grated cheese. Minced raw beef, liver or boiled fish can be given later on. By the time that it is one month old the kitten should be able to eat any food suitable for the cat family. It should be fed three times a day up to two months of age, then twice a day to four months, then once a day.

How to bring up a guinea pig

The cavy or guinea pig is one of the most charming household pets. If you want to make friends with one of these little animals always approach its cage with gentle gestures and avoid all sudden movements. If you pick one up hold it in the way shown in the illustration.

Give the guinea pig plenty of fresh vegetables, but make sure you remove all the leftovers in case they go bad for it is important that the bottom of the cage is clean.

The guinea pig loves maize, fruit, vegetables (especially carrots), lettuce leaves, and the core and peel of apples. If it gets plenty of vegetables it does not need to drink. It also likes a little bran.

The cage must be quite big so that the guinea pig can run up and down, and it should have a raised platform where the guinea pig can make its bed. The sawdust on the floor should be changed daily and the whole cage cleaned every week and disinfected about once a month.

During the summer the guinea pig can be put in a fenced-off part of the garden, but make sure that the fence is strong enough or the guinea pig will run away. Whenever it is allowed to wander freely about the house or in the garden, always make certain there are no cats or dogs about because they will attack it.

When guinea pigs are born they are already highly developed, furry, open-eyed and able to eat solid food. After only a few hours they can run about with their mother and are weaned in about two weeks.

The best way to hold a guinea pig (above) and a cat (below)

169

How to look after a dog when it sheds its fur

It is always an awkward time for dogs when they shed their fur. At such a time they should be treated gently and taken for long walks in the fresh air so that they can roll about in the grass and get rid of their loose hair. The dog should also be groomed with a metal comb so that it won't have to scratch itself too much, and brushed to remove loose hair and burrs. Short-haired breeds require little grooming but the longer the dog's hair the more it has to be combed. Some breeds have to be clipped regularly to maintain their health and good appearance.

The moulting period, when dogs shed their old hair, usually lasts about two weeks. During this period the dog should be given fatty foods containing butter, cooking fat or bacon fat. An average-sized dog can eat between 100 and 150 grammes of fat a day without being harmed but a safe fat limit is about 15 per cent of the dog's total daily food intake.

Cocker spaniel puppy

How dogs should be fed

The teeth of a dog are the teeth of a carnivorous, or meat-eating, animal, like those of the dog's wild cousin, the wolf or the fox. For this reason the more meat we give to a dog the longer it will live and the healthier it will stay. But we can also vary its food so that it receives two-thirds meat and one-third vegetables.

Dogs should be given nourishing meat either raw or cooked, in lumps or minced. The meat can be liver, tripe, fish, rabbit or chicken. Other food suitable for dogs includes broth, cheese grated over other food, an occasional raw beaten egg and a few teaspoonfuls of honey. At least once a week a dog should be given a lump of unsalted butter or fat. This fat in the diet helps to keep a healthy sheen on the dog's coat.

Dogs need large bones to gnaw from time to time for they are easy to digest and keep their teeth healthy. They should never be given splintery bones, though, such as those of chicken, rabbit or game. Neither should dogs be given salt but they need vitamin drops in their food.

Most commercial dog foods contain a balanced diet with all the necessary nourishment. If this is the dog's basic food it should be supplemented with small amounts of meat and fat.

Vegetable-based foods recommended for dogs include: rice broth seasoned with olive oil, vegetable broths or rice and milk broths, bread in small quantities and a little macaroni, carrots finely grated on to the rest of the food and occasionally fruit such as apple or pear. A few drops of orange or lemon juice can be added to the dog's drinking water.

Hamster

An ideal cage for a hamster

How to look after hamsters

The golden hamster, which is reddish-brown above and grey underneath, is one of the most popular household pets. It adapts very well to cage life but it is so tame that it can be let out to wander about the home freely. The hamster will let itself be picked up and stroked and will also answer when called by its master. In fact, it can be a real friend to children and keep them amused.

Twice a day the hamster cleans itself very carefully. A healthy hamster has thick, soft fur and no unpleasant smell.

The hamster also keeps its nest very clean. It always leaves its droppings in the same spot and throws them out of the cage if it can. When it finds food it stuffs it into the roomy pouches inside its jaws and then hides it in his nest.

When buying a hamster make sure the animal is young. Always buy two males unless you want them for breeding. Hamsters are very prolific, the female producing several litters a year. A young hamster has very flexible ears covered in fine hairs, bright eyes, a smooth, soft coat with no scars or discolorations.

The following are some rules regarding the care of hamsters.

If the animal's cage is small it must be fitted with a treadmill so that the hamster can exercise itself at night. A hamster needs to move around a lot and it can run as much as it likes on the treadmill.

A hamster will eat almost anything: bread, biscuits and small pieces of meat. But it also must have vegetables rich in vitamins such as carrots and lettuce. Another important item is grain food, including sunflower seeds.

It is not necessary to put a lot of food in the hamster's cage, especially if the food is perishable. The hamster hoards food in its nest and these reserves can go bad and cause infection.

How to prepare a bird-table

If you like birds and do not like to see them shut up in cages, you can still have the pleasure of watching them live in their natural state by setting up a bird-table for them.

To make a bird-table you need a long pole which is driven into the ground near a tree or shrubbery. Next you get a small box with low sides and nail it to the top of the pole to form a flat, horizontal surface for the birds to land and perch on. Some barbed wire wound round the bottom of the pole will stop cats from climbing up to the table.

What sort of food should be put on a bird-table? Breadcrumbs are not enough. There are two menus, one for birds that eat seeds and another for birds that eat insects. For the seed-eaters you need millet, barley, rice and breadcrumbs. For the insect-eaters you must have fat or minced meat, margarine, bread soaked in milk and bacon rind.

Perishable food such as meat, fat and milk should be changed frequently. Care should be taken not to frighten the birds because they may never come back again. Some insect-eating birds have the strange habit of eating in an upside-down position. For such birds put the food into a net which can be hung from a fence or a tree.

Birds need water to drink and to wash with and dishes of water should be put in safe positions so that the birds can splash about and enjoy themselves. Make sure you replenish the water supply every day or as often as possible. This is especially important in winter when natural supplies of water may be frozen.

How to make covered bird-tables for the winter

A small roof to the bird-table can stop food being covered by sudden snowfall in winter and provide birds with some shelter in cold weather. A similar roof can be built on the ground to cover the place where birds' food is usually put.

It is not too difficult a job to make such a roof and ordinary materials can be used. The easiest to make is a simple sloping roof and for this you need a piece of a broad plank. This can be kept in a sloping position on the ground by placing a pair of wooden supports at one end. The plank will provide a sheltered area for the birds and for their food.

Another simple type of roof can be made from two wooden boxes from which two sides have been removed. One of the boxes can act as a roof if placed at the top of a pole and the other as a platform or table.

The linnet has a light beak and therefore eats small seeds such as millet

The greenfinch has a strong beak which it uses to open up large seeds such as sunflower seeds of which it is very fond

How birds' food should be enriched in winter

Many people believe that breadcrumbs and a few grains of rice, corn or bird seed are enough to keep birds fed in winter. This is wrong. In winter birds need food with a high calorie content to fight against the cold.

When you put out food for birds in winter make sure you supplement it with nuts, bits of fat or bacon rind. You can make a sort of seed cake by mixing together the seeds, crusts of bread and other kinds of birdfood and binding it with animal fat. These seed-cakes can be placed on a window sill or in the garden. If you want to watch the birds eat you must not let them see you or they may be too frightened to come. Some birds, however, become very tame with regular feeding and will come every day and wait at the usual feeding place. Robins in particular are friendly birds who will approach people readily.

It is useful to sprinkle some sand around the food as it makes a more natural surrounding for the birds. Sand is also useful because birds usually swallow a few grains to help them digest harder seeds.

How to look after white mice

White mice are rarely longer than 10 centimetres from nose to tail. They keep moving about the whole time and you can watch them scampering about for hours in their cages without ever showing any signs of tiredness. One stops occasionally to nibble at some food but it soon starts moving restlessly about again. It likes the company of other white mice especially when it is young.

If you buy a male and female mouse make sure you have enough room for their young when they are born or else arrange to give them away or sell them to a pet dealer. You must avoid having too many of these animals and not knowing where to put them. As a rule, a male and female mouse can produce up to ten litters a year with about ten baby mice in each litter. In addition mice mature young, at about two or three months after birth, and then start producing litters of their own. This means that, in a relatively short time, your two original mice can found an extremely large family.

White mice will eat almost anything. Their best food, however, is a mixture of oats (ten parts) and millet (one part). This mixture should be made into a paste with water, and occasionally a small spoonful of cod liver oil or some vitamin drops can be added. Once a week give the white mice some fruit, lettuce or chicory. Do not give them any cheese. All waste matter connected with white mice must be removed regularly to avoid infection and disease.

How to look after terrapins

If you are going to have terrapins as pets it is essential that they are kept in a warm enough temperature. For this you need the kind of tank used for tropical fish. It should hold at least 20 litres of water for too little water can cause sudden temperature changes that may result in the terrapin catching pneumonia. A good temperature is between 20° and 27° Centigrade for many of these young terrapins are brought from

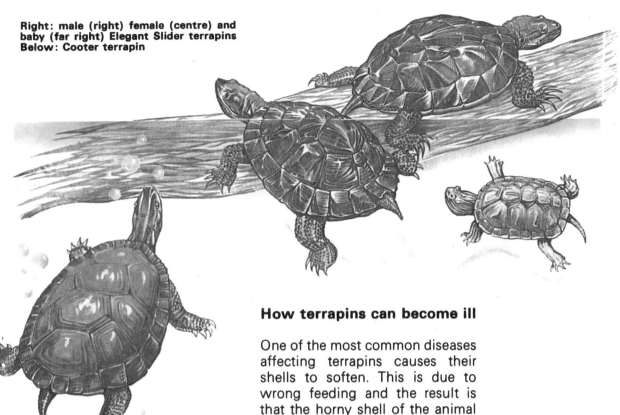

Right: male (right) female (centre) and baby (far right) Elegant Slider terrapins
Below: Cooter terrapin

How terrapins can become ill

One of the most common diseases affecting terrapins causes their shells to soften. This is due to wrong feeding and the result is that the horny shell of the animal becomes soft and pliable and sinks in at the top. This disease can be treated by giving the animal a varied and plentiful diet with lots of minced meat and vitamins.

Another illness in terrapins causes their eyes to become inflamed. This is often the result of the bottom of the tank being covered in sand instead of gravel or pebbles. As the terrapin swims around it stirs up small clouds of fine sand which go into its eyes and irritate them, sometimes blinding the animal. So always have gravel or pebbles at the bottom of a terrapin's tank to avoid this danger.

Baby terrapins are far more subject to these illnesses than adult animals. You should remember when buying terrapins that when fully grown they reach a length of between 17 and 20 centimetres.

the southern United States where they are used to a warm climate.

Water from the tap is chlorinated and although it is harmless as far as humans are concerned it is not good for terrapins. So tapwater must be kept in a bucket or a tank for a day. Chlorine is a gas and it will slowly evaporate from the water. You can also treat tapwater with filtration equipment.

Terrapin can eat the specially prepared food sold in pet shops but you must also give them chopped herring and raw, finely minced meat mixed with bonemeal and cod liver oil, but only a little at a time or it will rot in the water. Terrapins also like lettuce leaves and carrot tops. Give them a few drops of vitamin oil to help them stay healthy.

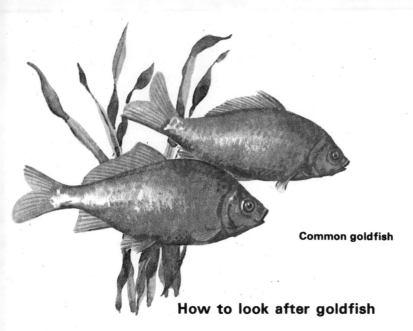

Common goldfish

How to look after goldfish

Goldfish make extremely popular pets. They are not difficult to look after providing you follow a few simple rules.

The first serious threat to a goldfish is when it is taken home from the pet shop. It should be swimming around in quite a lot of water and you should not take it in one of those small plastic bags. If you must use a plastic bag take the goldfish out of it as soon as possible or it may suffocate.

A second danger to goldfish is the tank it swims in. Tap-water contains chlorine which is poisonous to goldfish. This water is also too cold and might kill the pet.

A third danger is feeding which is all too often wrong for goldfish. These fish do not require much food, but what they do eat must be carefully chosen. Never give goldfish breadcrumbs: use the special food sold in shops but be careful to give it only in small quantities. Occasionally you can give goldfish a small amount of finely minced raw beef or the crushed yolks of hard-boiled eggs.

The larger the tank the happier the fish will be. The ideal tank is an aquarium but a large bowl will serve. Do not forget that even a goldfish can become bored and pine away living alone, so you should give it a companion, either male or female.

Goldfish were originally natives of eastern Asia but were later introduced into China, Japan, Europe and the United States. They have been known to live for twenty-five years in captivity, but the average life span is usually much shorter.

How an aquarium should be equipped

Only a few fish can adapt to life in the restricted space of a tank, but even these will die if they are not given the right surroundings.

The aquarium must be carefully prepared. On the bottom there should be a mixture of sand and pebbles to give a realistic look. Underwater plants are useful because they help to keep the water pure by absorbing waste products and providing oxygen. The water must be neither too cold nor too warm and it must not contain any harmful substances. It should seldom be completely changed or

replenished. A glass cover to the aquarium is often used, to reduce evaporation and prevent the fish from jumping out.

How frogs can be born at home

You have probably often seen frog-spawn in a pond. This spawn is a jelly containing tadpoles which are small creatures that grow into frogs. If you gather up some of this spawn and keep it in a large jar of water taken from the pond itself, the tadpoles will continue to grow by feeding on the microscopic plant life in the pond-water. You can add a few pieces of lettuce to the water as extra food.

When the tadpoles are a month old, little hindlegs develop and grow, and then forelegs appear. As the legs grow the tail gets smaller and at last disappears.

When the tadpoles reach the final phase of their development, put a sloping surface such as a board into the water. This will allow these animals to climb out of the water when their lungs develop and they have to breathe air.

It is extremely interesting to watch the tadpole gradually turn into a frog about 2 centimetres long. But be careful: frog-spawn is very much like that of other amphibians and the tadpoles might turn out to be toads or newts.

American leopard frog

European frog

Bull-frog with its spawn and tadpoles

177

List of Questions

The illustrations in this book are the work of the following artists:
D. Andrews, H. Barnett, M. Battersby, J. Bavosi, J. Beswick, R. S. Coventry,
G. Davies, Design Bureau Practitioners Ltd., D. Forrest, R. Geary, G. Green,
H. Green, N. W. Hearn, K. Lilly, D. MacDougal, A. McBride, M. McGuinness,
B. Melling, P. Morter, J. Nicholls, W. Nickless, A. Oxenham, G. Palmer,
H. Perkins, D. Pratt, J. Rignall, B. Robertshaw, M. Rutherford, M. Shoebridge,
J. Smith, B. Stallion, K. Thole, G. Thompson, P. Thornley, C. Tora, R. Wardle,
D. A. Warner, P. Warner, Whitecroft Designs Ltd., M. Whittlesea, J. W. Wood
and Associates, W. Wright.